# The Ocean World of Jacques Cousteau

## Riches of the Sea

# The Ocean World of Jacques Cousteau

## Riches of the Sea

ANGUS AND ROBERTSON

*The ocean offers far more than a **wealth of unexploited minerals** and untapped oil reserves. It is a new home for man where, if he treads gently, he can be nourished both physically and spiritually.*

This edition published by
Angus & Robertson (UK) Ltd.
2 Fisher Street, London WC1
102 Glover Street, Cremorne, Sydney
107 Elizabeth Street, Melbourne

Published by Harry N. Abrams, Inc.

Published exclusively in Canada by
Prentice-Hall of Canada, Ltd.

Revised edition—1975

Project Director: Steven Schepp

Managing Editor: Richard C. Murphy

Assistant Managing Editor: Christine Names
Senior Editor: Ellen Boughn
Research Coordinator: Robert Schreiber
Editorial Assistant: Joanne Cozzi

Art Director and Designer: Gail Ash

Associate Designer: Leonard S. Levine
Illustrations Editor: Howard Koslow

Creative Consultant: Milton Charles

Printed in the United States of America

12345678998765

LIBRARY OF CONGRESS CATALOGING
IN PUBLICATION DATA

Cousteau, Jacques Yves.
    Riches of the sea.

    (His The ocean world of Jacques Cousteau;
v. 17)
    1.  Marine resources.    I.  Title.
GC1015.C68      333.9      74-23068
ISBN 0-8109-0591-4

# Contents

When man was just THE CLEVER PREDATOR (Chapter VI), hunting with rudimentary tools, his food-gathering methods were not likely to deplete the ocean's living resources. The rules of his societies and religions often forbade excessive exploitation of the sea. The earth's population was small; food needs could be satisfied without taxing the ocean's supply even as knowledge of fish behavior made fishing more efficient.

As societies grew into huge nations, they justified massive takes of fish by creating THE FOOD MYTH (Chapter VII). It was a commonly held belief that the ocean had an infinite capacity to supply food to the world. As fish-catch figures diminish, it becomes apparent that only through careful regulation of fishing quotas will the sea continue to meet even limited food needs. If the human population is not held in check, controlled fishing will not be possible: starving, overly populated nations are not likely to respect strict fishing quotas.

As an alternative to fishing we look to FARMING THE SEA (Chapter VIII). Through the techniques of mariculture, we can replace what we take from the ocean and create new hardy breeds of marine life that will mature faster. Natural populations of marine organisms will be left to replenish themselves without man's interference. Like the advent of agriculture, ocean farming could change the outlook of mankind. For the first time in hundreds of years, we have the opportunity to develop a new food source.

Controlled culture of marine plants and animals will make available a MARINE MEDICINE CHEST (Chapter IX), stocked with a constant supply of raw materials from which new drugs with exciting possibilities can be produced. Every toxin and poison in the sea has potential as a medicine. Antiviral and antitumor compounds have already been isolated from marine sources.

Finally, we understand that the sea's greatest treasure is not a monetary one. A SEA OF RECREATION (Chapter X) exists to provide enjoyment, fresh challenges, and an opportunity to replenish creative wellsprings. The ocean's ability to soothe and stimulate is of foremost importance to twentieth-century man seeking relief from the pressure of living in overcrowded cities where the beauty of nature is notably absent. The intellectual stimulation available in great urban centers is a vital aspect of a full life; but in order to fully participate in that life, we must be able to escape occasionally into a less hectic pattern. The sea provides such an escape.

# Introduction: Manna from the Sea?

When mathematicians entered a new field of speculation just by deciding that an imaginary number would have a negative square, it sounded like a harmless exercise. But while the improbable hypothesis was extending the scope of abstract thinking, it was also set to work in electronics, helping to develop transistor radios—and devastating guided missiles. Advances in science, however pure in their intentions, are always available for possible uncontrolled applications.

Aesop's "tongue parable" should help remind us that men can use anything for the best or for the worst. Science originally was intended to increase our understanding of the universe, but it opened doors inadvertently to deadly, as well as helpful, inventions. Technology was meant to increase the quantity of goods available in order to satisfy essential human needs, but with still one-half of mankind in want, new needs were wildly created. Diverted from its objective—the quality of life for all—technology has given rise to a dangerous myth: quantity for the sake of quantity; more goods, even if they satisfy only artificial needs, even if they are unevenly distributed; more energy, even if most of it is wasted; more money, even if it is devalued in a mad monetary race. Today a nation's importance is measured by its rate of production rather than by its intellectual contribution, by its gross national product rather than by its artists and composers. With increased production the only goal, the responsibility of nations to the environment and to future generations is abandoned. The emphasis is on "more" rather than "better." We have ignored the wisdom of Mies van der Rohe's statement: "Less is more." Today the word "progress" is used as a synonym for "growth." And growth grows out of hand, unchecked, like a tumor on mankind.

Our very minds are so contaminated that when explorers open the gates of the ocean or of outer space for mankind, we ask: What resources do the moon and sea have to offer? How can we exploit them—quickly, if possible? This book will partially answer such questions. But it is essential to discuss what a reasonable approach should allow us to expect.

Mass slaughter of whales, incessant scraping of the North Sea's bottom with heavy trawlnets, killing of porpoises and dolphins in huge tuna purse nets, ravages of coral reefs by spearfishermen, hasty oil drillings in unsafe offshore areas—these are examples of how a distorted image of progress can lead to a shameless rape of the sea. We must not wait for obvious warnings—like the imminent collapse of industrial fishing—to switch to a rational, internationally controlled management of marine resources. These resources will be more than sufficient to allow us the time needed to check the world's population, reconsider the priority of needs to be satisfied, and better allocate the planet's wealth.

Before the turn of the twenty-first century, fishing will be progressively replaced by mariculture. With offshore oil reserves almost exhausted, mining the ocean floor will provide a bounty of ore for several useful metals. New drugs such as antibiotics will be extracted from marine creatures. But the greatest material contribution of the sea to man's welfare will be in the field of energy. Our present Western civilization depends on coal, oil, and natural gas —three fossil fuels that are nothing more than energy from the sun, transformed in plants and plankton in an extremely low-efficiency process, stored up through many millions of years. It is high time to find more direct access to the sun's power; but the major problem is that even in deserts, where heat is concentrated, this energy is scattered over huge areas. In the sea, on the contrary, the sun's energy is *naturally* concentrated in certain areas: in ocean currents, to some extent in tides, and maybe even more inexhaustibly in the temperature differences between the surface and the deep waters in tropical zones. Marine thermal plants of gigantic proportions could provide massive quantities of electricity for the production of liquid hydrogen, the clean fuel of the future. Such plants will also generate artificial upwelling currents and thus fertilize the surface of the oceans.

Having acknowledged our past mistakes on land, we are being handed a new world in which to demonstrate new-found abilities to exploit without greed and without pollution; to colonize without conflicts; simply to contemplate and create. The greatest riches are those of the heart, and the sea is capable of literally flooding us with aesthetic and intellectual joys.

Jacques-Yves Cousteau

9

# Chapter I. Sunken Treasure

Since ships have sailed the sea, some have failed to reach their destinations. Storms, uncharted rocks, naval battles, and pirate raids have all sent ships and their crews to the bottom. Captains have even been known to scuttle their own vessels for a profit. Every time a ship sinks, it becomes a possible sunken treasure trove.

Spanish galleons that brought gold and silver from the New World to the treasuries of Europe in the sixteenth and seventeenth centuries are the sunken vessels that most modern-day treasure buffs dream about. They often fail to realize that very accurate records were kept of Spanish ships, and salvage operations were started immediately after the news of a wreck reached land. Of

---

> "Most sunken ships that went down in water beyond the range of the free diver still sit there awaiting discovery."

---

course, the salvagers had scanty tools in those days, but we have a tendency to underestimate the performances and efficiency of native divers. However, modern divers have been able to take fortunes from wrecks that had been salvaged 10 or 15 times in the past using equipment inferior to today's.

In the past, few attempts were made to salvage ships that went down in deep water beyond the range of the free diver. These ships, for the most part, still sit on the sea floor awaiting discovery.

Spanish galleons are not the only treasure ships to have sunk into the sea. In the Mediterranean are vestiges of ancient Phoenician, Egyptian, Greek, and Roman vessels, some of which surely carried African gold. Asian porcelains and other riches were brought by

sea on the Manila route to South America. Thus Chinese treasures lay trapped on the floor of the South Pacific. Wherever the sea was used as a highway for trading vessels, some ships still lie on the side of the road.

One of the world's first trade routes was across the Indian Ocean. Sailors were quick to learn that they could sail one way with the monsoons and return with the opposite winds the next season. Wrecks no doubt occurred on the route. If remains of these ships, which sailed before the time of Christ, are at the bottom of the Indian Ocean, it is likely that they would be of more interest to the archaeologist than to the treasure hunter.

Locating sunken treasure is hard work, a lot more difficult than the child's dream of finding a lost map marked with an X. Sometimes years of research precede a search. Manuscripts written in ancient languages must be deciphered; expensive reconnaissance missions must be mounted. Even if the treasure is found, the lucky finder is rarely the keeper. A French citizen, no matter from what area he salvages a wreck, must turn over 100 percent of the booty to his government and the government alone decides upon the compensation. Spanish and Portuguese government regulations state that ancient ships that once flew the flags of these countries still belong to them. If a wreck is located off the coast of Florida within territorial seas, the state demands a fourth of the treasure. But even against these odds, some men still get an itch in their palm and a "Long John Silver" glint in their eye at the mere mention of the magic words "sunken treasure."

*Cannon and ballast stones* are often the only indication that a ship lies buried in an area. Obvious ballast stones mean nothing is left of the hull.

# Silver Bank

In the summer of 1643 the flagship of the Spanish Silver Fleet, a galleon called *Nuestra Señora de la Concepción*, crashed on the treacherous reefs of the Silver Bank north of Hispaniola, the island in the West Indies that is now divided into Haiti and the Dominican Republic. With the ship went a treasure trove of pearls from Venezuela, gold and silver from Mexico and Peru, and various jewels valued at over $3 million in today's currency that had been destined for the coffers of the Spanish king. During the years that followed, the booty from the ship enticed men from many nations to risk their ships on the same reef.

William Phips was a Bostonian ship's carpenter whose ambitions went beyond those of his impoverished family. By the time he was 23, he was on his way to trade in the Caribbean on his own ship, *The Star of Boston*. During his Caribbean wanderings, Phips often heard tales of shipwreck and treasure. Many Bermudians were making well known the amounts of silver and gold they were taking in salvage operations. The story of the *Nuestra Señora de la Concepción* came to Phips by way of one of her survivors, an old man that Phips befriended. Treasure

*A seventeenth-century **map of the Caribbean** shows the areas crossed annually by the Spanish fleet. The path taken by the ships often brought them close to dangerous shoals in the hurricane belt.*

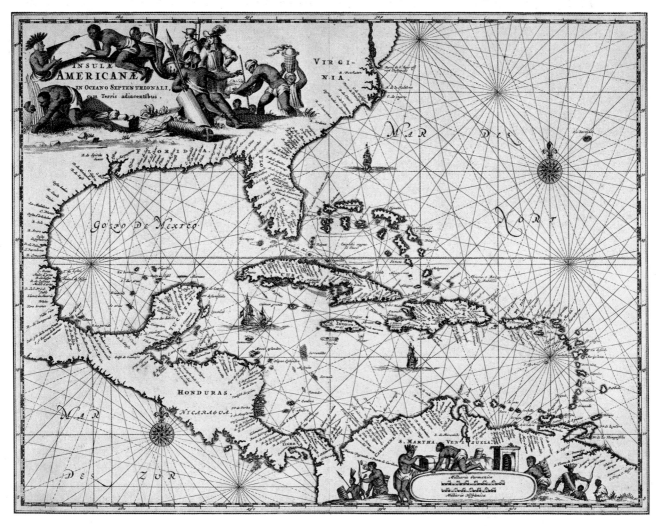

fever seized the former Bostonian, and he sold *The Star of Boston* to buy passage to England in order to seek a patron in his venture to raise the wealth of the Spanish ship.

He obtained the financial backing of no less a dignitary than the king, Charles II. *The Rose of Algiers* was outfitted, and Phips set sail immediately for the "silver bank" as the reef was known. A lengthy search yielded nothing but a solitary silver ingot imbedded in a sea fan. The crew became discouraged and attempted a mutiny, finally sending Phips scurrying back to England, where he found that Charles had died.

Phips was unrelenting in his search for support and was able to gain the confidence of the Duke of Albemarle and the new king, James II. Two ships, *James and Mary* and *Henry of London*, left England in 1686.

Phips was not a dim-witted fellow as some of his biographers have claimed. He carried English goods on the *James and Mary* and proceeded on a trading mission to establish in the minds of the gossiping islanders that he was in the Caribbean for business not

*Ships on the bottom are soon **encrusted with coral overgrowths**, making their discovery a challenging task. The treasure itself is often hidden within the core of a coral clump.*

treasure. Meanwhile the crew of *Henry of London* began the search. Within days the adventurers found some silver bars, and then the galleon itself in six fathoms of water.

Phips was sent for and work began. For six weeks they worked the reef, always keeping an eye out for pirates. When a supply ship did not return within an allotted time, Phips feared that news of the find had leaked out. He prepared to return to England. In the holds of the two ships were chests filled with pearls, rubies, gold, and silver. The final take was measured by the king's men to be 27,586 pounds of silver, 347 pounds of plate in precious metals, 25 pounds of gold, and great quantities of pieces of eight and jewels. Phips was given $75,000 and made governor of Massachusetts as his reward. However, like many treasure seekers, he found that his wealth could not buy happiness. He died penniless before his forty-fifth birthday.

*Collecting basket (top) is floated to the surface by filling drum with air.* **Suction hose** *(bottom) removes sediments, exposing artifacts.*

*An air lift is manipulated by a diver (opposite). Debris is collected in a basket. A crust of coral may conceal a fused clump of silver coins.*

## Caribbean Treasure

After the voyages of exploration that began with Columbus, the Atlantic became a well-traveled highway. In the decades that followed, Spain began to bring the wealth of the New World to Europe on regular routes that her ships sailed along. Their holds, heavy with Aztec and Inca treasure, were too tempting to be ignored for long. Pirates soon became a danger that appeared with greater regularity than the dreaded hurricanes. In the mid-1500s, the ships of Spain began to gather together in flotillas for protection against thieves at sea.

Once a year Spain sent two fleets to the New World to carry supplies for the colonists and bring back the wealth. The *Galeones de Tierra Firma* sailed to Colombia, where its ships were loaded with gold, emeralds, and pearls. Enough room was left for silver transshipped from Peru. The other fleet sailed to Veracruz for Mexican gold, pieces of eight, and fine porcelain and silk that had traveled from Manila to Acapulco and overland to the Mexican port of Veracruz. Each year in June the fleets massed in Cuba to make the Atlantic crossing before the hurricane season. An eighteenth-century manuscript describes the fleets: "The King of Spain, whose dominions are now extended from the east to the west, whose kingdoms are fully a third of the known world, whose treasures in his western dominions are rich and durable mines of gold and silver . . . without bottom or a seeming end, from which flows the wealth of Spain . . . yearly sends his mighty ships of Spain into America which moving road bring him home his annual treasure of gold and silver."

The fleets didn't always get underway in time to avoid the hurricane season. Often a ship crashed on one of the many Caribbean reefs in a heavy gale. One estimate says that the number of shipwrecks from the days of the galleons through the present totals over a thousand, all resting in the fairly shallow waters of the Caribbean. The ships that avoided devastation by tropical storms were not guaranteed a home-safe journey to Spain. They had to slip past sleek pirate ships with cunning captains whose spies let them know which ships were the most apt to carry gold. Encounters with these outlaws sometimes caused the galleons to founder as they struck out over unfamiliar territory to evade the skull and crossbones.

Many of the wrecks have been picked at by salvage crews from time to time. Others are nothing more than monuments to a small chapter in the history of navigation and hold wealth valuable only to the archaeologist. Some may have gone down when they were bringing supplies from England in the nineteenth century and certainly don't contain gold or silver. Others are from the recent past, carrying little of value. But the possibility of locating a rich find still exists. Millions of dollars wait under the sea for a knowledgeable adventurer to find.

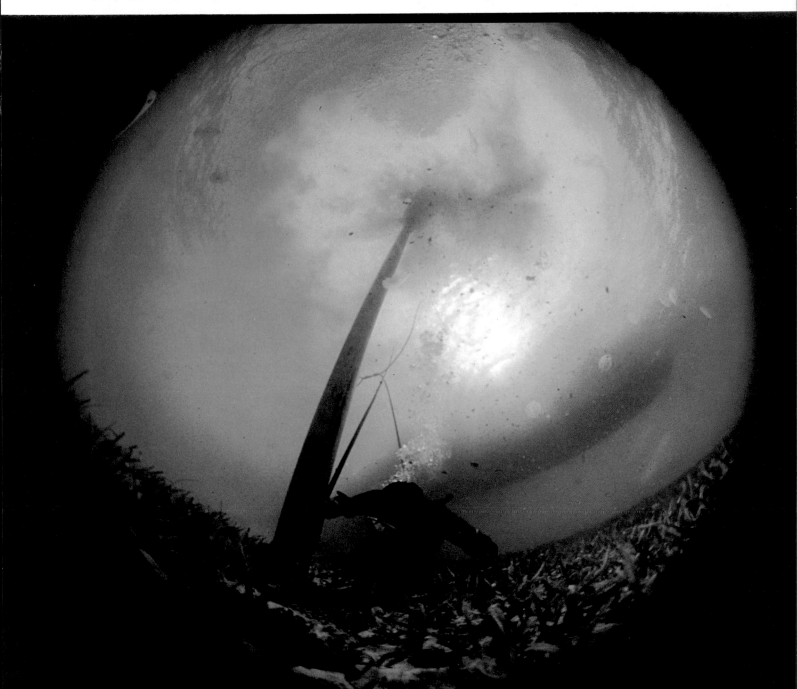

# Egypt's Gold

In May 1922, in a heavy fog off the coast of Brest, a British liner, the *Egypt,* collided with another ship. Her radio operator sent SOS signals for 20 minutes before the ship went down, taking most of her crew and passengers with her. In the *Egypt*'s vault was over $6 million in gold and silver. Even though land-based radio operators picked up the *Egypt*'s signals and the ship that collided with her returned for survivors, the exact location of the wreck was not known.

The lure of the $6 million sent fortune hunters with many odd salvage schemes to Lloyd's of London for years after the catastrophe. Lloyd's had paid on the *Egypt*'s insurance and was eager to recover its loss.

The major problem facing salvage crews, if they could locate the ship, was water pressure. Divers using traditional compressed-air methods of the time could not go as deep as the *Egypt* was suspected to be. An engineer, C. P. Sandberg, who proposed using German-designed pressure-proof diving armor that was safe to 700 feet, was finally awarded the *Egypt* salvage contract by Lloyd's. He was to get 37.5 percent of the value of any recovered cargo. Sandberg hired an Italian salvage firm headed by Giovanni Quaglia to carry out his mission.

First the wreck had to be found. Trawl lines were drawn across the ocean bottom in the vicinity of the wreck. When the lines hooked on something, a man was sent down in the heavy German diving gear to look around. For two years, whenever weather would permit, the diving team searched for the *Egypt;* When frequent Atlantic squalls prevented

*Salvage of the* Egypt *was accomplished by a man in an observation chamber who directed the placement of dynamite charges and guided the mechanical grab into position.*

the search teams from going out, they practiced the use of their diving equipment on a wreck in shallower water from which they salvaged Congo ivory. Finally, two years after the *Egypt* search began, the drag lines hooked her bow. She was over 425 feet down.

Salvage was a long, drawn-out affair; the treasure vault was in the very bowels of the ship. Because the diving bell and salvage equipment were suspended from the surface, they had virtually no lateral mobility underwater; the vault could only be entered from above. This meant several decks had to be stripped away before the vault could be exposed. A diver was lowered in the diving chamber and directed the placement of dynamite charges on the wreck. The diving bell was then retrieved, and the charges detonated. Then a mechanical grab was lowered to lift away pieces of the hull that had been torn away by the blast.

Just as progress was being made, the entire diving crew was killed, and the tender ships destroyed, by a blast on another wreck. During 1930, the crew had been engaged in the removal, by blasting, of the *Florence,* a ship that had been sunk by German submarines. The salvage ship was sunk by her own blast. Replacement of crew and equipment took a year's time. Toward the end of the summer of 1931, the treasure vault aboard the ship was penetrated. Before any of the spoils could be retrieved from the storeroom, winter descended and the wreck had to be deserted for six months. When the men returned they found that the hole from which the gold had been seen had filled in. At last, four years after the initial search, the electronic grabber pushed through the jammed opening and brought the first gold bullion to the surface. Three years after that, the last of the $6 million was fished from the sea.

# Treasure Today

Finding sunken treasure is an enterprise far beyond just childish fantasy. A Florida corporation has made tidy sums in each of the last 10 years from gold and silver that went out of circulation 200 or 300 years ago.

The Real Eight Company was formed as the result of a hurricane. The same force that sent many a rich galleon to the bottom brought a silver coin, stamped with the Spanish seal, to a Florida beach one morning in 1955. The beachcomber who found the coin was so excited by the possibility of locating more of them that he formed a treasure-seeking corporation that specialized in the wrecks of one Spanish fleet—that of 1715.

The War of the Spanish Succession delayed the sailing of the Silver Fleet for over two years, from 1713 to 1715. When they finally set sail from Havana, laden with two years' collection of riches, the combined armada of 1715 carried $14 million in treasure. The traditional June departure date was delayed. When the fleet finally set out on July 24, it was the hurricane season.

*Cannon* (top) *and ballast stones* (bottom) *are examined by diving scientists. The cannon's size prevents it from becoming hidden by coral.*

*A recent wreck* (opposite) *provides more clues to the diver than older ones. The sea has not yet concealed the general outline of this ship.*

The sky was clear as the 11 ships pulled into the Gulf Stream to roll past the Florida Keys. At 2 A.M. a hurricane roared down, smashing the ships one by one on the ragged reefs off what is now Cape Canaveral. Only one vessel, a French ship that carried no treasure, survived. Salvage crews were immediately sent out under the Spanish flag. Millions of pesos of the cargo were retrieved by divers and returned to a camp on shore. At least 1 million pesos of the treasure was returned to Havana before pirates attacked the land camp and put an end to the salvage.

Kip Wagner, the founder of the Real Eight Company, began his search for the remains of the Silver Fleet of 1715 by searching for the base camp along the Florida coast, as a hobby. At first he picked at the sandy coasts with a shovel. Finally, after three years, another glint in the sand caught his eye. A large, crudely made gold ring set with an enormous diamond lay at his feet.

The next step was a reconnaissance mission over the Florida bay in a rented plane. Wagner knew that he wouldn't see an entire ship under the waves—the wooden structure would long ago have ended up in the bellies of teredos (shipworms). He was hoping to see ballast stones, all that usually remains of a ship long at the mercy of the sea. A suspicious dark blotch on the reef was finally spotted from the plane and the Real Eight Company began in earnest to find the armada of 1715.

The first four dives yielded pottery, of interest only to museums. On the fifth dive, pieces of eight were found. A dredge and water jet were moved in to remove sand. As clouds of sediments and shells moved to one side, the divers were amazed to see thousands of golden doubloons exposed on the ocean floor. The Real Eight Company located all 11 of the fleet's vessels and has brought up over a million dollars in gold, silver, and jewelry.

# Chapter II. Mining the Sea

The ocean is said to be a vast storehouse of natural resources. Successful exploitation of the ores and minerals from the sea depends upon three factors: expansion of geological knowledge to facilitate the location of resources; technological advances to enable pollution-free extraction and mining; and definition of international law regarding marine mineral rights. The last of these goals is critical to the other two: if neither national governments nor private industry can be assured of legal protection for their investment, they will be reluctant to locate or develop marine natural resources.

International law, like all other systems of rules governing the activities of individuals, grows out of claims and disputes between human beings. Whenever a question of ownership arises, rulings from the recent and remote past are called upon to help define the rights. But laws relating to the ocean have

---

**"Technology has altered our ability to take from the sea. Also we have come to realize that ocean mining can pollute other marine resources."**

---

usually been concerned with navigation and fishing, since technology did not reach a level to make mineral rights in the sea an issue until the last few decades.

In the early 1960s the International Law Commission of the United Nations proposed that the land and resources of the continental shelf belonged to the coastal nations. The high seas were free for exploitation, but recommendations were made for the pollution-free use of these waters. Other groups have proposed different solutions. One suggests that the open sea is the common property of mankind. Large countries would be trustees of small ocean areas, while small countries would have rights to large portions of the sea. The United States' position has been that exploitation should be confined to the continental shelf, which should be patrolled by an international committee other than the U.N. Many industrial interests regard the ocean from a "gold rush" standpoint: the ocean's mineral resources belong to whomever first stakes a claim—a dangerous philosophy.

If it had not been for two factors—technology and awareness of pollution—the law of the sea would today remain as it was defined in the eighteenth century. Technology has altered our ability to take from the sea. And we have come to realize that mining and shore activities can affect the ocean resources of all nations by pollution. Now that we understand that our capacity to ruin extends to the open sea, international law is struggling to define both responsibility and control measures for pollution-free mining in the ocean. An international law of the sea conference held in Venezuela in 1974 has attempted to define both these points. But some countries have no shorelines; why should they be deprived of the ocean's resources? The sea is beginning to teach us that there is only one world for one mankind and that the old concept of nations is maintaining almost intolerable legal segregation. The world desperately needs the ocean's mineral resources, but they must not be exploited at the risk of further international turmoil or destruction of the ocean itself.

*Ocean mining ship,* the Glomar Explorer, *owned by Summa Corporation prepares to sail for the Pacific Ocean. In its mining operations it may gather huge quantities of valuable manganese nodules from the sea floor.*

gineering, Inc., Washington, D.C., working with Matachewan Canadian Gold, Ltd.

The first step that these modern prospectors took was to study the onshore ore deposits of Nova Scotia. These geological patterns were related to offshore sediment movement and sea-bottom topography. Marine areas, like buried stream channels or ancient beach lines (places where water has been at work separating and concentrating heavy metals), were selected as likely drill sites. Core cuttings from the drills were returned to a research vessel via a vacuum pump. The scientists then passed the cuttings over a sluice box much like those used by gold miners over a hundred years ago to extract nuggets from Alaskan streams. Three areas of significant gold deposits were found offshore.

*Nuggets brought downstream from rich veins can be taken from shore or directly from the stream bed (left). A diver (below) holds a golden nugget.*

## Gold Rush

"Thar's gold in them thar hills"—so the prospector said when begging for a grubstake to help him make a claim in the California gold rush. Today it could be said that there's gold under the waves, at least the ones that lap the shore along the Atlantic seaboard of Nova Scotia. Several substantial marine deposits of gold have been discovered by a unique drilling method in a joint undertaking by Ocean Science and En-

When gold was discovered in the Rocky Mountains in the nineteenth century, the cry spread over the land, causing towns to spring up overnight. The discovery of gold in the sea has not caused such excitement, and a marine gold rush has not taken place for several reasons. The land prospector needed only a pick and shovel to start his search. Ocean mining poses much greater problems. The largest deposits of marine gold were found beneath 14 to 21 fathoms of water. The mechanics of getting the gold out are complicated and expensive. A Canadian company has developed a suction dredge that scrapes the underwater area to bedrock. Gold-bearing material is drawn onboard, where the gold is extracted and the tailings returned to the sea. But such a system severely disrupts the life of the organisms that live in the dredging area on the continental shelf. Offshore mining challenges technicians to discover methods that will not seriously interfere with bottom-dwelling plants and animals, either by smothering them or poisoning them with toxic wastes.

Gold may be found underwater in any area where streams that yielded high rates of gold feed into the sea. Deposits similar to those off Nova Scotia have been located near Nome, Alaska. Apparently the vestiges of the great Yukon strike are still there—in the ocean. A large international oil company began a seismic study of the offshore topography in 1960. In the winter of 1964 they moved a large drilling rig out onto the ice and took core drillings of the sediment that had filled old streambeds. They haven't disclosed what they found, but soon after the drilling was completed, they leased over 5000 offshore acres. Speculation is that the area could yield 300 tons of gold at a profit of $50 million. Since the value of gold has increased greatly in the last few years, this figure may be on the low side.

**When dredging a stream bed,** the nuggets are drawn up and screened from gravel and other matter by sophisticated "panning" methods.

## Manganese Cobblestones

The *Challenger* Expedition was the world's first global oceanographic survey. When the *Challenger* returned to England in 1876 after several years at sea, she brought back enough information to fill a 50-volume set of books. On a few pages of one volume mention was made of baseball-size nodules of manganese that had been brought up in the deep-sea dredges from various oceans. Several theories to explain nodule formation were proposed by crew members.

No further attention was given to the odd mineral deposits except as curiosities until the early 1960s, when the extent of the deposits became known through underwater photography. Some seabeds looked like cobblestone streets, so heavily were they paved with the nodules. In some areas the concentration of the nodules reaches 180,000 tons to the square mile. Manganese nodules could even be a renewable resource. It is thought that the nodules may be forming at the rate of 16 million tons per year in the Pacific Ocean. But it is not known whether or not

present harvesting techniques will alter or destroy the circumstances that cause the nodules to form.

The nodules usually contain other materials, such as copper, nickel, and cobalt. The process by which the nodules are formed is not clear. Shark's teeth or fish earbones have been found at the core of some of the nodules, leading researchers to suggest that they may precipitate out of a supersaturated solution of minerals. One idea is that the minerals collect due to the action of certain bacteria —an enticing idea since it suggests that the nodules might be "raised" on a mineral farm.

Several methods have been suggested for mining the nodules. The two most reasonable ones are the use of deep-sea hydraulic systems or of a cable-bucket system. The hydraulic techniques depend upon a dredge to collect and sort the nodules on the ocean floor. Then they are drawn up by an air lift to the surface for collection. The cable-bucket system is just what it sounds like. A series of collecting containers is attached to a cable that moves them down and across the ocean floor. They are pulled up and emptied.

Several companies have entered the nodule-mining field. A subsidiary of Tenneco has been working on a mining system since 1963. After completion of sea trials in 1970, the mining ship *Deepsea Miner* proved that her air-lift dredges could do the job. Uncertainty about the legal aspects of deep-sea mining has cooled the project somewhat. The legal questions were taken up by the first United Nations Conference of the Law of the Sea held in Venezuela in 1974.

One company—the Summa Corporation—has gone ahead without regard for the eventual legal ramifications of its work. Its techniques for deep-sea mining are said to be more advanced than any so far proposed. These have been incorporated in the Summa flagship, the *Glomar Explorer,* built behind guarded barricades in Philadelphia by subcontractors, the Global Marine Company. The ship has completed sea trials and, after final fitting of dredges and pumps that are capable of bringing up 5000 tons of nodules per day to the surface, will probably begin working the eastern Pacific floor. A measure of the potential worth of the nodules is seen in the $70 million investment the Summa Corporation made in *Glomar Explorer.*

*The* **Glomar Explorer** *(opposite, top), an experimental vessel, can lift industrial quantities of manganese nodules from the deep-sea bottom. The nodules form around smooth objects such as sharks' teeth. The shape of the nodule determines its name.* **Cannonball nodules** *(opposite, bottom) and* **grape nodules** *(below) litter the floor of the Pacific.*

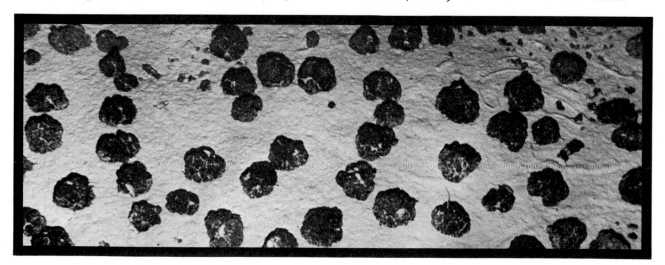

## Expensive Water

Water may yet prove to be the ocean's most valuable resource. As the world's population increases, water supplies are being wasted and depleted faster than they can renew themselves in a world where rivers are systematically poisoned. If we continue to pollute our natural freshwater system, desalinated seawater may fill our growing needs.

Sodium chloride, common table salt, accounts for the greatest percentage of material by weight dissolved in seawater. Over 44 other components are also found in seawater. Isolating fresh water is easy on a small scale. When water evaporates, it leaves impurities behind. This is a slow process when allowed to occur naturally.

The most conventional way to increase the speed of evaporation and to collect fresh water from salt water is by distillation. The water is boiled and the steam collected.

*A desalination plant (above) extracts fresh water from the sea by speeding the evaporation process.*

*Man-made salt flats (below and opposite) trap ocean water. Salt stays behind, is processed and sold.*

When the steam contacts a cool surface, it condenses as fresh water. But great amounts of energy are required to convert a steady supply of water by this method. Expensive water is the result.

Nature uses solar energy to produce fresh-water supplies. Man may do the same in the future. An experimental solar still was sponsored by Prince Albert I, and constructed in Monaco at the turn of the century. A peaked glass roof covers a trough of seawater. Heat from the sun is trapped in the structure much as it is in a greenhouse. The water vaporizes and collects on the glass roof. Although solar stills are not in common operation, distillation methods of various types, including nuclear heat sources, account for the production of millions of gallons of fresh water.

Hot, moisture-laden tropical winds may be induced to give up their freshwater supply by being brought in contact with a cold surface. The only source of cold in the tropics is the deep sea. Thus bottom water could be pumped up to cool the breezes so that they would drop "rain" into collecting pools.

The most peculiar idea proposed to draw fresh water from the sea is to bring icebergs north from Antarctica to melt in collecting barges off the shores of thirsty countries. Bergs would be located by satellite and hooked into tug-propelled chains. Scientists estimate that only 20 percent of each berg would melt during its journey to New Zealand or Chile; less would survive the trip to the Northern Hemisphere.

The "impurities" that desalinization attempts to remove from seawater are of great value in themselves. They include bromine, sodium chloride, and magnesium. Research is underway to devise methods of extracting these minerals in conjunction with the production of fresh water. Extraction of these elements at the same time would make desalinization less expensive.

# A Girl's Best Friend

Poetic descriptions of the sea often make a comparison between the play of sunlight on the waves and the sparkle of diamonds. Off the west coast of South Africa, millions of dollars worth of diamonds litter the seabed.

It has long been suspected that the set of volcanic conditions that made the African coastal area rich in diamonds may have caused them to spill out into the sea. Underwater exploration for the diamonds was not undertaken, however, because of the economics of mining in a coastal sea that rages and boils up against a rugged coast so dangerous that it's called the Forbidden Coast. An adventurous Texas pipeline builder, Sam Collins, was the first to extract diamonds on a commercial scale from the gravel that covers the seabed. He converted a few barges to dredging vessels, which were called Collins's Follies, and began to work the offshore area. His operation was not totally successful. A series of mishaps, including the loss of his main barge, left the business in poor financial condition. Collins's limited success attracted the attention of big miners to the possibilities of underwater mining.

Collins was eased out of the operation and his equipment was replaced with a grotesque, but beautifully functioning diamond-mining barge, *Pomona*. She works in conjunction with a tug and two support and sampling vessels called *Rockeater* and *Bellatrix,* designed for prospecting missions. *Bellatrix* carries out limited mining operations with suction hoses maneuvered by divers. When an area proves rich, large-scale dredging is taken over by *Pomona*.

*Pomona* has a much larger crew than any of the other vessels in the diamond fleet—114 men live on board. She anchors over a likely area and maintains her position by means of a tellurometer—sea-to-land measuring equipment. Suction hoses are lowered into the sea to depths of up to 100 feet. Gravel and the diamonds are pumped to the barge by air-lift and suction dredges. The diamonds are sorted by filtering screens against which they are driven by pressurized water jets that also clean the jewels. Oversized (marine diamonds are small) and light particles

*The final step in recovering diamonds from the sea is **hand sorting** (opposite and above). The gems are picked from gravel of the same size.*

*The main diamond mining vessel, Pomona, works in conjunction with several **barges** (top) that carry on limited mining with **suction hoses** (right).*

are returned to the sea. The remaining material is sorted again by hand and the diamonds, between 0.4 and 0.5 carats each, are recovered. Around 12,000 carats of diamonds are taken each month.

Extensive new diamond fields have recently been found off the coast of Africa near a group of small islands called Roast Beef, Plumpudding, and Guano—unlikely names for the origin of a girl's best friend, but a likely place to reap a sizable profit.

## Dredging for Sand and Gravel

All that doesn't glitter isn't necessarily worthless. Sand and gravel must be the dullest of the ocean's resources, especially when contrasted with oil, diamonds, and gold. However, to societies that depend upon cement for construction material, sand and gravel are almost as valuable a commodity as any in the sea. From a tonnage standpoint, sand and gravel are the most important resources that we mine from the sea. In so doing, we turn immense areas of marine nursing grounds into biological deserts.

In Great Britain the island's land sources of gravel are close to being exhausted. Presently 15 percent of the total tonnage comes from the sea. It is projected that in England all gravel and sand will come from marine sources within 15 years.

The British gravel industry is carried out by 32 different companies that are operating more than 75 seagoing hopper dredges that range from 300- to 10,000-ton cargo capacity. Cost of obtaining the gravel is only 35 to 50 cents per ton. Wholesale price ranges from $1.00 to $3.00 per ton.

In the United States gravel and sand constitute a billion-dollar-per-year industry. Growth rates projected to the year 2000 estimate that the demand will increase fourfold. Two factors cause industry planners to look to the sea for their future needs. First, land supplies are becoming depleted just as in Great Britain. Second, increased public concern over land-based gravel operations has resulted in environmental restraints on the industry's terrestrial operations.

Stress is obviously already heavily put on offshore organisms by increased dredging

monwealth of Massachusetts has relaxed its moratorium on offshore dredging in order to facilitate the study. Detailed biological and ecological data of the area will serve as the baseline against which dredging damage will be assessed. Then we will witness a lobbying contest between the industrial and the fishing pressure groups; life in the sea is at the mercy of such shortsighted struggles.

Several other products (aside from gravel, gold, and diamonds) are mined by dredging the continental shelf. Calcareous shells, useful for their calcium carbonate for cement and fertilizer, are mined from deposits in the Gulf of Mexico and off Iceland. Tin is taken from ancient riverbeds that lay under the sea in Indonesia, Thailand, and Malaysia.

*As land resources are exhausted, more and more* **gravel barges** *(opposite and below left) dredge the continental shelves for this valuable resource. In the process,* **giant scoops** *(directly below) wreak havoc on the marine environment.*

of their environment. Dredging the continental shelf turns entire marine provinces into disaster areas. Plant life and fixed fauna, as well as shellfish and crustaceans, die as silt, stirred up by the dredging, settles over them. Eggs and larvae of an untold number of species are destroyed. Since it seems inevitable that the industry will exert increased pressure to expand further into the sea, the National Oceanographic and Atmospheric Administration (NOAA) has undertaken an impact study of offshore gravel mining in Massachusetts. They have selected a site, rich in the resource, and are mining with a 30,000-ton hopper dredge. The Com-

Running down the center of the ocean basins are divergent areas, and material coming up from the center of the earth is added to the sides of two plates as they move away from each other. This game of cosmic musical chairs is, of course, time-consuming, taking place over aeons. In a time when it is often difficult to relate what happened yesterday to today's events, such vast periods of time are hard to conceive. But corollaries of the theory of continental drift are giving ocean prospectors some solid guidelines to finding mineral deposits in the ocean.

The **rift valley** (above) on the Mid-Atlantic Ridge shows evidence of plate drift.

The **bathyscaphe** Archimède (opposite) is currently assisting in a massive study of plate tectonics in the Mid-Atlantic Ridge.

## Geological Movements

Deciphering the origin of the earth and the great geological events that followed is a travail that rivals the quest for the Holy Grail. But the task is not as difficult as it seems because all over—both on the land and under the sea—are planted clues to the puzzle. In the past five years many pieces of the puzzle have been tied together to give credence to a theory that the continents were once connected. According to the theory of continental drift, they came into their present position by the spreading of the sea floor between the great landmasses.

Critical to the theory is the idea that the crust of the earth is composed of many plates, from 6 to 23. The boundaries of the plates move in three ways relative to each other. At convergent boundaries, one plate reenters the interior of the earth by sliding beneath another. In some earthquake-prone areas, the boundaries slide in opposite directions, parallel to each other.

At the places where one plate dives under another, minerals emanate from the converging plate as it melts into the earth. These molten minerals then combine with sulfur to form metallic sulfide deposits. The Kuroko deposits of Japan, the sulfide ore veins of the Philippines, and the rich metal deposits in former convergence plate areas, such as are found in the Rocky Mountains and the Andes, are examples of this phenomenon. Localities where plates diverge, commonly found in midocean regions, are also important areas of mineral formation.

The Red Sea is considered young when we speak of oceans. A divergent area is spreading the sea floor between the continents of Africa and Asia. Discovery along the center of the Red Sea of rich metallic sulfide deposits in sediments and in solution in hot brine pools directly above the sediments has sent scientists scurrying to see if similar concentrations of metallic sulfides appear in older ocean basins. Veins of copper located by deep-sea drilling at a depth of 7380 feet beneath the Indian Ocean indicate that other "old" oceans may hold similar deposits.

# Chapter III. Black Gold

The world's use of oil has increased from 11 million barrels daily in 1950 to 46 million today. Seventy percent of the oil and natural gas is consumed by the United States, Canada, Western Europe, and Japan and the majority of it is used for transportation. The fact that many countries in South America, Africa, and Asia are rapidly becoming industrialized means that as long as no change is made in the priorities of our civilization, worldwide oil consumption will continue to increase and soon reach unreasonable levels until nuclear or solar systems can be safely developed. Political problems in the Middle East, the world's major source of fossil fuels, and petroleum transportation difficulties have caused many nations to look into further exploitation of their own underdeveloped reservoirs. In most cases, land areas have been tapped. Only the offshore and deep-sea oil sites remain to be exploited. More than a million dollars *per day* is being spent along the U.S. Gulf Coast alone in the search for and development of offshore sources of oil.

Currently over 2 million square miles of gas and oil areas in Europe and North America are being prospected by over one hundred national and private petroleum companies. Hundreds of deepwater or offshore drilling units are operating. Problems of deepwater drilling that were insurmountable just 15 years ago are being solved by an industry geared for expansion. The result of much research and development activity has been a more secure flow of oil. (Indications are that gasoline shortages of 1973 in the United States did not reflect the true status of unrefined reserves.) Much of the technological advancement made in the oil industry has been made against the protests of individuals and organizations concerned about the environment. It becomes obvious after the latest Middle East crisis that a reasonable management of the irreplaceable oil reserves of the world calls for drastic reductions of all unnecessary and wasteful uses, such as heavy, overpowered cars carrying only one or two passengers on crowded highways where speed is not limited.

In 1968 the United Nations issued a questionnaire to its member nations in an attempt to get a worldwide perspective on

> ## "Over a million dollars is spent daily to develop offshore oil in the Gulf of Mexico."

pollution: over half the respondents cited oil or gasoline as the major source of pollution in their nation. The expansion of offshore drilling and wider use of the automobile in many nations since that time have no doubt increased the complaints.

The International Convention for the Prevention of Pollution of the Sea by Oil has been in existence since 1954. Its regulations prohibit discharge of oil (due to bilge flushing) within 100 miles of shore. Even so, 5 million tons of oil are spilled into the sea every year. Since the series of oil spills in the late 1960s, the petroleum industry has made some attempts to protect the ocean from the effects of its undersea work. Additional precautions have been made against tanker collisions and accidents. But an industry that spends millions to further its exploitation of the sea should make more than token efforts to protect the world's resources.

*Oil rigs* need not be unattractive. Off Long Beach, California, oil wells masquerade as apartment structures on an offshore artificial island.

# Oil Prospecting

Locating undersea oil reserves is not a perfected art. Geological theory that evolved from land exploration led to the first offshore drillings in Louisiana. Today an army of geologists, aided by the tools of technology, roam over suspected fields with a fairly high chance of locating oil.

The process by which oil is formed is still not clear. The generally accepted theory is that marine organisms are trapped in areas where oxygen levels are low and decay bacteria can not break down the organic structure of the plants and animals. The hydrocarbons produced by this partial decay collect in layers of porous limestone or sandstone. The oil may float above a layer of water that prevents it from migrating downward. It must be sealed from upward movement by an additional layer of impermeable rock that overlays the deposit. Oil-yielding rock is often as-

**Oil platforms** (above) placed high above the forces of the sea are protected from storms and have given a boost to ocean-mining procedures.

**Oil** has been discovered off the coast of a peaceful Nigerian village (below). The village may be destroyed by the machinery of the oil industry.

A stretch of **southern California beach** (opposite) was once a sanctuary for shore life. Today, insensitive development has spread ruin.

sociated with large deposits of salt, called salt domes, that can be located by seismic studies. The nature of the bottom and subbottom topography can be determined by the use of sonar. Profiling aids, such as explosions that further expand the sonar readings, can reveal the geological structure of the ocean bed to at least 2000 feet below the ocean floor. Eventually, after an area has been identified as having possibilities as an oil field, samples are taken by core drills.

A massive research project with a well-equipped ship at its disposal is presently collecting data to further ease the task of the oil hunters. The ship, the *Glomar Challenger,* is a 10,000-ton deep-sea drilling vessel that is capable of telling scientists more about the history of the earth——and the location of oil and minerals——than has ever before been possible. The *Glomar Challenger* does not belong to an oil company. It has been given financial support by the National Science Foundation and is managed by Scripps Institution of Oceanography. On her maiden voyage the vessel brought back major findings. The first surprise was traces of oil and gas found under 12,000 feet of water and 500 feet of subbottom material in the Gulf of Mexico. This is the first time that oil has been found in a deep-sea area.

The *Glomar Challenger* had to be designed to stay above the drilling area within a few feet, without interference from wind or sea. Slight variations in its position could cause the heavy drilling machinery to be ripped from the bottom or from the ship. The remedy is called dynamic positioning. The vessel is equipped with omnidirectional "thrusters" capable of counteracting the forces of wind or currents wherever they come from. These thrusters are instantaneously activated by a computer that receives very accurate information about the ship's drift from sonar beacons placed on the bottom.

*Multiple rigs* are able to drill a number of productive wells from a single platform.

## Oil on Troubled Waters

Once an oil field has been located and off-shore leases negotiated, the organization involved begins the expensive process of moving in its drilling rigs. About half of the rigs working offshore fields are "jack-ups." These are floating rigs that are towed to the site. Then, their "legs" are extended to the bottom, and the entire rig is raised high above the turmoil of the crashing waves. This type of rig can be used only at depths of 300 feet or less with any degree of stability.

For deep-sea drilling, floating rigs are required. There are two types: a surface vessel like the *Glomar Challenger* (or a modified ship) and a semisubmersible platform. The latter has been developed to overcome the problems of maintaining a floating vessel in an exact position on the moving surface of the sea. It is a stable, ballasted platform submerged to the ideal level for drilling in a particular area. Once the well has been tapped, the platform rises to the surface and is towed to a new site. These floating derricks cost from $5 to $10 million.

Once exploratory drilling has been completed, the newly tapped well is fitted with equipment to facilitate production. At shallow depths, it is most common for a stationary superstructure to be anchored to the ocean floor to provide support for the well heads, oil-gas separators, tankage, and other facilities. In deeper water stationary platforms are too expensive. Systems have now been designed to provide undersea working areas for divers so they can install well heads and pumping stations on the ocean floor to service deep-sea wells.

Most of the newly designed oil production equipment and transportation vessels are somewhat protected against accidental spillage. However, in most cases the protection is inadequate. As was so dramatically illustrated by the *Torrey Canyon* oil tanker accident off England in 1967, when over 35,000 tons of oil escaped onto the sea, oil spillage is in no way a thing of the past. The petroleum industry has come up with several ways of partially controlling, containing, and dispersing oil spills if they do occur. Prefabricated, polyurethane barriers can be constructed around a spill area to prevent oil from invading harbors or estuaries. Once the spill is contained, it must be picked up and transported to a disposal place. The pickup can be accomplished with some degree of effectiveness by suction nozzles or mechanical skimmers that work like big rotating sponges. At the time of the *Torrey Canyon* incident, the only hope was the use of detergents, which proved to be a greater detriment to life than the oil. In areas where detergents hadn't reached the shore, limpets disposed of the black goo by eating it. In detergent-sprayed areas the limpets died.

Some studies funded by oil companies on the *Torrey Canyon* and the Santa Barbara, California, oil spills have shown that the effect on marine life was not quite as destructive as was once thought. Waterfowl are the main victims of oil on the sea since they must pass through the sticky stuff to get to their food. Life along the shoreline has been reported to recover with minor long-term effects. In contrast an independent study of the east coast found significant, long-lasting effects of oil on life.

***Elevation of drilling rigs*** (right) *high over the ocean's surface on jack-up supports* (below) *has somewhat diminished the possibility of storm-related oil spillage from offshore drilling equipment.*

# Troubleshooting

Extremely expensive sets of equipment are now humming away all over the world, extracting undersea oil. The well-being of a machine that costs per day the equivalent of the yearly salary of a teacher is of utmost importance to the petroleum industry. Consequently, an offshoot of the mining of oil has been the development of an array of equipment for monitoring and servicing the underwater aspects of the marine oil industry.

Underwater television has been adapted to guide the installation of well-head equipment. Remote control "robots" have been in use since the early 1960s to help guide the

*Expensive delays occur when a **drilling rig** (left) breaks down. Divers save time by spotting flaws.*

***Conshelf III divers*** *proved to be (below and opposite) an asset to the petroleum industry. An underwater drilling rig was assembled by them.*

drilling. Some cases simply require a man on the bottom. Our Conshelf project, in which men worked as deep as 370 feet under the sea, illustrated that underwater man was capable of servicing an entire drilling rig. Manned submersibles or special guided capsules can take over when the location is too deep for diving men.

Waiting until a critical part breaks and causes an entire operation to slow down or stop completely can be an expensive gamble. Remote-control surveillance of submersed rigs has been designed to protect delicate machinery from breakdown. Inspection operations are common. Oil companies whose rigs are not equipped with computerized surveillance devices use submersibles to make periodic inspections of their equipment.

In fact, the petroleum industry has given great impetus, both theoretically and financially, to the development of working submersibles. In most cases the oil companies have farmed out their vehicle work to subcontractors, aerospace companies which have moved into the underwater market. When the oil company needs a sub for inspection duties, it leases the machine and its attendants from the owner.

Our understanding of deep-diving physiology—how man's body reacts to deep dives—has been greatly enhanced by the aid the petroleum industry has given in their search for ways to man underwater oil rigs where conventional diving equipment is useless.

The industry has given a boost to other areas of research. Mapping of the ocean floor was stimulated by interest in locating new oil reserves. The results have been significant in aiding oceanographers. Much of what is now known about the geological structure of the sea, seabed, and subbottom can be traced directly to seismic studies carried out and financed by petroleum companies.

## Manhattan's Odyssey

The location and tapping of a marine oil well is only the first of many steps necessary to get the refined products to the consumer. Transportation of crude oil is often difficult because of the great distance between oil field and refinery. Major oil fields have recently been discovered on Alaska's north slope, but the transportation of this rich find poses enormous difficulties.

Two solutions have been put forth by the oil companies to solve the problems of getting the crude oil to refineries in southern Alaska and then to markets in the United States. The most feasible proposition, to the oil companies at least, is the construction of a pipeline across the state. The pipeline has encountered great opposition from environmentalists for several reasons. The oil in the pipeline will be of a high temperature. Since the line will rest on the permafrost, it is thought that the heat will eventually melt the frozen earth, causing the support under the line to give way where the subsoil is unstable. This would increase the chance that the pipe will sag and break, spilling oil into the earth at a rapid rate. Second, Alaska is earthquake prone; a major quake could also sever the line. It is thought that the migration of caribou and other wildlife might also be interrupted by the melted permafrost around the line.

As an alternate plan, all major oil companies with interests in the north-slope find financed the $40 million round-trip voyage of a refitted and reinforced supertanker, *Manhattan,* between the East Coast of the U.S. and Point Barrow, Alaska. If the *Manhattan,* with the aid of her icebreaker escort, could make the trip through the ice-clogged Northwest Passage, she might open the way for an entire fleet of supertankers to make regular trips from the north slope. Starting in the

summer of 1969, the *Manhattan* crashed her way to Point Barrow, and in early November she completed her 11,000-mile round trip. Resting on her deck as she pulled into New York harbor was a golden drum of crude oil, symbolic of her mission.

The voyage of the *Manhattan* was a technical success. However, a fleet to travel the Northwest Passage has not been constructed for several reasons. Primarily, the idea of a northern tanker fleet was shelved because

the pipeline won congressional support after a long and bitter contest. Navigation of the icy waters was accomplished, but not without great difficulty. Ice intrusions that resemble reefs were encountered throughout the voyage. Charting the ice "reefs" is a mammoth task yet to be undertaken.

Transportation of oil from less-remote areas is not much easier than getting it down out of the north. Supertankers which can carry oil at a cost much lower than that of smaller vessels are in operation. In the United States only the ports of Los Angeles, Long Beach, and Seattle are deep enough for very large crude carriers (VLCC). Creation of new, deep harbors is opposed in most areas by the public, which fears oil spills will be a result of VLCC harbors. Offshore "sealine" terminals could solve this problem.

*The* **Manhattan** *crashes through the ice to open water on her northern voyage from Alaska to the Atlantic and the eastern United States.*

# Chapter IV. Pollution-Free Energy

The use of fossil fuels (gasoline, coal, oil, and the like) as a major energy source is far from an ideal method of obtaining power. To start with, the world reserves of fossil fuel will sooner or later be depleted, leaving us short of supplies of coal and oil for some other major fields such as the petrochemical industries. An educated guess puts the earth's petroleum supply at about 6 trillion barrels. We are presently using this supply 100,000 times faster than it took nature to produce it. Further, the mere transport of oil, for example, can have disastrous effects on the environment as oil spills from damaged tankers have so dramatically illustrated more than once in the past decade. Air pollution, which ends up finally in polluting the oceans as the atmosphere is

---

> "The need for pollution-free energy is causing us to look to the sun and sea for answers."

---

washed down by the rains, would not be eliminated if major industries ceased to burn fossil fuels; the contribution that automobiles make to bad air is much more significant. However, if gas, coal, and oil could be replaced for industry and power plants by alternate energy sources, it would have a considerable positive effect on the quality of air and water.

An apparently cleaner supply of energy is nuclear fission. Since domestic sources of uranium are greater than those for oil and gas, most new power sources in the future will be nuclear-powered electrical generation plants. Critics of atomic systems, however, are quick to point out that uranium supplies are also finite; a University of Massachusetts scientist has estimated that obtaining uranium could be a problem by 1990. Nuclear fission plants require natural supplies of water for cooling. If too many plants are constructed, the ability of rivers, lakes, and tidal waters to absorb warm effluents may be overtaxed and further damage rendered to aquatic and marine life. It is estimated that the other main nuclear type of reaction, fusion of hydrogen into helium, will not be practically available before the twenty-first century.

Ten years ago energy supplies in the United States came primarily from a mixture of fuels: coal, oil, natural gas, and uranium. Only 3 percent derived from hydroelectric sources. In the face of the power versus pollution problem and increased needs for pollution-free electricity, we can once again look to the sun and to the sea for answers.

In 1971 a group of faculty members and students at the University of Massachusetts tackled the problem of creating a nationwide network of pollution-free energy systems. Of the six innovative sources they identified, four depended upon the sea. In a paper presented to the National Science Foundation, the group pleaded that the high costs of non-polluting systems be measured against the *pollution* costs of the old methods.

In their final paper, the university team suggested the development of power-generating systems that use the tides, currents, and waves. They suggested the use of electrical production from ocean temperature differences. In each case, care was taken to examine the possible damage to the sea from the proposed systems. There will be little.

*Harnessing the power of a **surging wave** would create considerable pollution-free energy. The idea is still waiting for practical solutions.*

# Tidal Power

Through the miracle of photosynthesis, plants can transform the sun's energy into food that animals can use for a variety of purposes including movement—another form of energy. No living system, except man, can harness the gravitational energy of the moon to use as a power source.

It has been known since ancient Greek times that the tides were related to the moon. The earliest reference to a method for capturing the rhythmic surge of the tides was in the Domesday Book, a chronicle of all British financial holdings undertaken by William the Conqueror in 1086. By the late Middle Ages tidal mills were in existence all along the coasts of England, Holland, and Wales. Richard Careu described them in *Survey of Cornwall:* "Amongst other commodities afforded by the sea, inhabitants make use of divers creeks, for gristemilles, by thwarting a bancke from side to side, in which a floudgate is placed with two leaves; these the flowing tyde openeth, and after a full sea, the waight of the ebbe closeth fast, which no other force can doe: and so the imprisoned water payeth the ransome of dryving an undershoote wheele for his enlargement."

The first tidal mill in the United States was built in 1635 at Salem, Massachusetts. It, like all the mills previously mentioned, used waterwheels, low in energy production compared to the only modern contrivance that harnesses the power of the tides to generate electricity on the Rance River in France.

The essence of the Rance project is 24 novel turbines that catch and heighten the energy of flowing water. As the tide moves in, blades

*The dam that bridges the **Rance River** in France contains 24 highly specialized, electrical generating turbines. This project is the world's most successful in harnessing the tides.*

on the turbine are turned by the water's motion and electricity is produced. At the highest tidal point, the turbines become part of a dam that blocks the water in a basin. As the tide ebbs, a head is created. Then the turbine gates are opened. The water rushing back to sea again generates electricity. The unique turbines can also act as motors. When electricity is fed into them, they drive pumps that increase the tidal flow and, hence, overall output. The turbines are housed in a structure beneath the plant. When the machinery needs repair, divers enter a hatch and descend to service the equipment.

Such generators can be constructed wherever great extremes exist between the level of high and low tides. At the Passamaquoddy arm of the Bay of Fundy in Nova Scotia, the tidal range is 50 feet, one of the greatest in the world. As early as 1919, engineers proposed designs for a joint U.S.-Canadian power plant for Passamaquoddy. Franklin Roosevelt finally gave his approval to the plan, but it was halted by engineering and political difficulties. Revived in the 1960s by John F. Kennedy, it again failed to receive congressional approval. However, the U.S. Army Corps of Engineers continues to update the plan in the event the energy crisis makes it imperative to turn to tidal power as the only alternative to fossil fuels.

There are a few drawbacks to the construction of tidal river power-generating facilities. The least critical is that the blockage makes the waterway inaccessible to commercial and pleasure craft. Scenic pollution also occurs; turbines and dams visually mar the beauty of a river. Life cycles of shore and marine organisms may be affected by changes in water salinity, temperature, and nutrients. Finally, extensive dams would cause a very slight decrease in the speed of earth's rotation. These are relatively insignificant compared to the damage done by other systems.

# Windmill in the Gulf

Before the advent of electricity, windmills dotted many farmlands. The power of a swift breeze would turn their blades and pumps would be driven to pull water from underground wells. Today, a worldwide electricity grid has rendered these wind-driven pumps obsolete in most parts of the globe. Yet, one of the most imaginative methods of capturing the power of the seas uses the antique principle of the windmill.

The waters of the Gulf Stream quickly flow past the Florida Keys. The force of its kinetic energy equals that of a swift breeze. The speed of the current fluctuates with the seasons but is always more constant than the most reliable winds. These facts have lead physicists to propose a system of underwater "windmills" that would run on the power of the Gulf Stream.

Within the core of the stream, in an area 10 miles wide and 450 feet deep, running for 350 miles off the U.S. coast, the velocity of the water is strong enough to drive rotor-type machines. It is proposed that a row of 12 turbines abreast be spaced a mile apart for the 350-mile stretch. Over 100,000 megawatts of pollution-free power would be produced. Late in 1973, the U.S. government approved plans to pursue the project.

Temperature differences between the warm Gulf Stream and the surrounding waters may be put to work to create yet another method of extracting electricity from the Gulf Stream. A system that exploits temperature differences between surface and bottom waters had been tested by the French

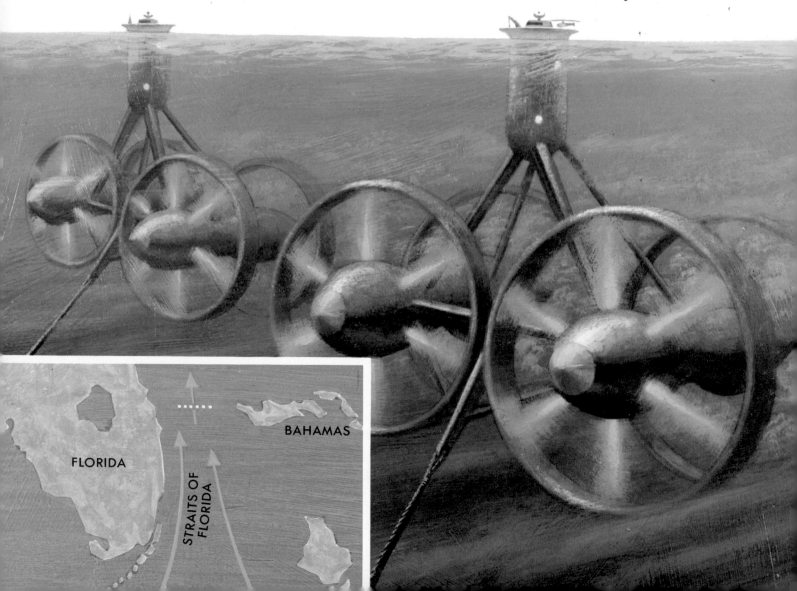

FLORIDA

STRAITS OF FLORIDA

BAHAMAS

pioneer Georges Claude as early as 1929 in Cuba. Surface water that has an average temperature of 82° F. is channeled into a vacuum-type boiler where it becomes steam which is used to drive turbines. The steam is then cooled by contact with 46° F. seawater that has been pumped from the ocean bottom. This causes the steam to condense and creates a vacuum to draw additional steam from the warm surface water to drive the turbines.

It has been estimated that 82 trillion kilowatt hours (kwh) of electricity could be generated annually from thermal gradients just in the Gulf Stream. These are heartening figures when posed against the anticipated need for 2.8 trillion kwh in all of the United States for 1980. The proposals for thermal gradient heat engines in the Gulf Stream plan to use the speed of the current to move warm water through the boiler and to inhibit the growth of fouling organisms on the machinery. Only one side-effect of the process seems to exist. Cold bottom water released at the surface could interrupt some biological activity. It seems unlikely that this will occur and bottom water may increase the productivity of the area by artificial upwelling.

*Giant blades* drive turbines in an artist's representation of a pollution-free generation system. The kinetic energy of the Gulf Stream is transformed into electricity. Tethered to the ocean floor, each dual-blade system would feed its electricity into a collecting grid that would deliver the power to land-based transformers and, then, to distant industrial centers. A team at the University of Massachusetts envisions a nationwide network that would tie the Gulf Stream to five other nonpolluting sources.

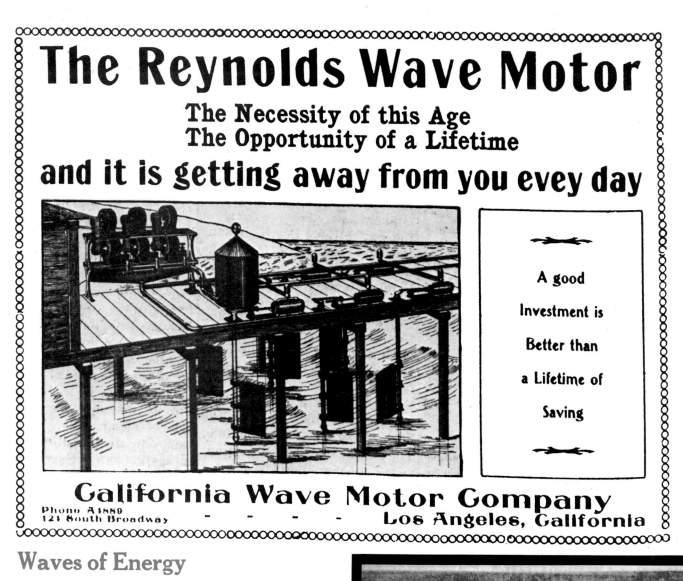
## Waves of Energy

In 1909 a new invention called the Reynolds Wave Motor appeared. Its designers claimed that it could transform the energy of the pounding surf into electricity. Panels were suspended into the water where they caught the force of the swells and transmitted it to a wheel that drove a generator. The yield of electricity was sufficient to light strings of bulbs but not much else. Eventually the contraption washed away in a storm, and the idea faded into oblivion.

The theory was sound though, and recent technological developments indicate that it may be the basis for an efficient power system. The energy that surges erratically across the seas is immense. A four-foot wave

is estimated to have 5.45 horsepower per wave; that is, 28,000 horsepower per mile. A greater ratio of power is inherent in taller waves. If the power in one 10-foot wave was harnessed for the distance of one mile, it would equal one-quarter of the daily energy output of a typical nuclear generation plant.

Several electrical generation systems based on wave energy have been patented in recent years. The one that is receiving the most attention is capable of large-scale production of electricity. Concrete troughs lined with hydraulic fluid encased in rubber would be placed near shore. As a wave crashes into the trough, pressure extended on the hydraulic fluid would be transmitted to shore.

The United States Senate, stimulated by a resolution introduced in 1970 by John Tower, a Republican from Texas, undertook a study of the "tides" (waves) as an energy source. In speaking for the resolution, Sena-tor Tower said, "Our government should avail itself of existing knowledge on tidal . . . energy as part of its function as overseer of environmental quality." Turning to the potential that traditional generators have for wreaking havoc, Tower said that development of marine generators would help combat thermal pollution, which "is equally as dangerous as air and water pollution."

Large-scale production of electricity from the waves awaits in-depth research. But a system not too different from the 1909 Reynolds motor is now on the market. A motor is placed 20 to 30 feet out from the shore. Water swishes into one part of the machine, churns three sets of paddle wheels, and flows out while turning three more wheels. Only about 5000 watts of electricity is generated per wave, but the inventors feel that the system will provide clean, cheap power for remote island communities.

*A 1909 advertisement (opposite top) announced a system to generate **electricity from the ocean's waves.** The machinery atop a southern California wharf (opposite below) generated only the interest of crowds of onlookers.*

*A modern version of **a wave motor** (below) is capable of producing modest amounts of electricity. Its inventors admit that even a greatly enlarged model could not light a large city, but the system may prove adequate for small island communities.*

## Floating Power

Nuclear power remains the least polluting of any present-day method of generating electricity. As we await the efficient harnessing of power from the tides and currents, the ocean contributes to the usefulness of nuclear energy in several ways.

There are two basic waste products from nuclear reactors. One, warm water, can be destructive to temperature-sensitive plants and animals. But mariculturists are putting the warmth to work in coastal ponds to hasten the rate at which plaice, sole, and shellfish grow and to enhance their survival.

The second class of by-products from nuclear power plants is potentially much more dangerous. These are radioactive isotopes. The ocean, according to some, dilutes radioactivity with greater ease than does land. They say that since the sea environment is rich in chemicals, the ratio between radioactive isotopes and their nonradioactive counterparts is smaller in the sea than on land, where fewer chemicals of all types exist. The theory is logical only at first examination. The oceans being the "end of the line" for any land-based source of wastes, radioactivity would soon pile up to intolerable levels. Furthermore, radioactive substances are unfortunately subject to bioconcentration and would be returned to us in our food fish. Sealed containers of radioactive wastes have been sent to the bottom of the sea and deep-sea photographs have shown many of the containers damaged and leaking. Again, it cannot be said that this is a safe method: anyone that has witnessed the ocean's ability to break up man-made objects knows that nothing remains sealed forever in the sea. The International Atomic Energy Commission oper-

ates a laboratory at Monaco to monitor radioactive waste in the sea. Hopefully they will convince politicians of the danger of dumping radioactive materials in the ocean.

Nobody wants a nuclear power plant in his backyard. The New Jersey Public Service Electric and Gas Company, with the combined efforts of Tenneco and Westinghouse, plans to construct the world's first floating nuclear power plant 2.8 miles off the coast of New Jersey. The developers believe that the open sea will disperse the warm water outflow with less damage than occurs when the heated effluent is dumped into coastal areas. But the warm water effluents will have to be kept at zero level of radioactivity, under very strict independent control.

It is apparent that the surface of the sea is, itself, a natural resource for a space-starved land. The U.S. Federal Aviation Administration is considering the design of floating terminals, and several groups are involved with floating cities. The utilization of the ocean surface far from land areas for power plants, airports, cities, and resorts reduces the threat of destruction of coastal estuaries and wetlands. These are areas of very high biological productivity: their nutrient-rich waters provide food and protected habitats for the young of many commercially important fish species. The continued filling in of wetlands to build beaches, hotels, and industrial sites can only have a detrimental influence on the survival of animals that depend upon wetland areas during early stages of life. If such structures are built offshore, delicate coastal ecosystems can be protected. The benefits will be seen in increased catches of species that thrive in estuaries—nature's nurseries.

*Nuclear reactors* (this page) require water as a coolant. *Atomic power plants* like this one (opposite, top) at San Onofre, California, could be moved out to sea where hot water effluents would not be as damaging to sensitive coastal organisms.

53

# Chapter V. For the Connoisseur

The unique and the rare as well as oddities and curiosities have always captured the eye, and the purse, of the wealthy. From the sea come some of the world's most prized collectables, giving pleasure and profit to the connoisseur. Hardly a culture exists that doesn't cherish some item from the sea.

The legendary cloth-of-gold from antiquity came not from underground mines but was spun by marine bivalves known as pen shells. These molluscs secrete byssus fiber, a milky substance that hardens into bronze threads which the animal uses to anchor itself. Byssus was first woven into cloth in the Kingdom of Colchis on the Black Sea. Jason and the Argonauts called the elusive golden fleece "Colchis," giving rise to the modern theory that the fleece was made from byssus. Today, the visitor to Italy can purchase gloves and scarves cut from cloth-of-gold but may be

---

*"The modern connoisseur seeks fabulous treasures in the sea but does not look for murex or cloth-of-gold. He seeks instead novel foods and rare shells."*

---

disappointed to discover that the most prized cloth of the ancient world resembles sleazy rayon more than elegant silk.

Until the advent of synthetics as a fixative in perfume, a substance produced by sperm whales was a necessary ingredient for all expensive perfume. Ambergris, from the intestine of the sperm whale, adds a subtle odor to perfume and extends the time that the smell lingers. The substance serves no known purpose for the whale. It was once thought that it was regurgitated only by sick animals, but this does not seem to be a correct assumption. Another theory is that ambergris is gen-

erated as an intestinal defense of the sperm whale when the undigested beak of a giant squid happens to perforate its stomach lining. When a mass washed up on a beach, it was collected and made small fortunes for lucky beachcombers. Today, its value has decreased since only a few of the finest perfumes still rely on it as a component.

Battles have been fought, families destroyed, and history made by man's desire for jewels like the pearl. Perhaps the first nation to grow into world fame and financial power because of a luxury item from the sea was Phoenicia. The Phoenicians discovered that the murex snail harbored a dye that would turn silk a delicate shade of purple. They developed the art of dyeing cloth and carried their purple product to Greece and Rome. Thus arose "royal purple," since only the highest members of ancient communities could afford robes made from the cloth. Purple robes today remain a symbol of royalty in Europe. The demand for the dye exceeded the source, and the murex disappeared from the eastern Mediterranean, leading Phoenicians to travel farther out to sea in search of the snail.

The modern connoisseur seeks fabulous treasures in the sea but does not look for murex or cloth-of-gold. Instead he searches for novel foods, beautiful and rare shells, and "red gold"—coral. As the world population, the general affluence—and consequently the demand—grows exponentially, all these natural refinements, without exception, are seriously endangered. We urge the hobbyist to halt collection of these items.

*A French diver's treat can be a **dinner of violets,** a variety of sea squirt. Violets taste strongly of iodine and are believed to increase virility.*

## The Gobbling Gourmet

Practically every creature that creeps, swims, or crawls in the sea is relished by the Japanese. An ancient Shinto prayer reveals a list of ocean foods: "things that dwell in the blue-sea-plain, the broad of fin and the narrow of fin, seaweed from the offing, seaweed from the shore . . ." There is no such thing as a Japanese seafood restaurant—every table, humble and high alike, is graced with food from the sea each day. Japanese eat whale and sea urchin, octopus, and eel. Altogether, they eat nine marine mammals, sixty-three species of sea fish, eight kinds of shellfish, three varieties of clams, and two of shrimp.

*A French fisherman (above) offers **sea urchins and violets** (sea squirts) for sale. **Sea urchins** are cut open (below) to expose the tasty orange gonads. **Tourists** (below) enjoy a lunch of violets and urchins. Raw violets are scooped from their tough outer covering with the thumb.*

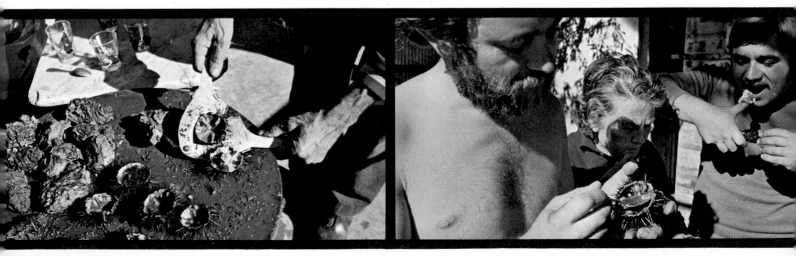

The Japanese enjoy raw fish, especially in a preparation called sashimi. The consumption of raw fish is repugnant to most Westerners, but once they have tried sashimi, their distaste usually turns to delight. Filet of tuna, sea bass, or any one of several other fin fish is sliced in geometric chunks and arranged in an appealing design. The diner grasps a chunk with chopsticks and dips it in a sauce mixed from soy sauce and wasabi —a hot horseradish paste. The flavor of sashimi is anything but raw. The taste is so delicate and the texture so smooth that sashimi is often the first food eaten by patients just returning from the hospital. Sashimi has won many devotees in the West and is always a popular entrée on the menus of Japanese restaurants in other countries.

One of the finest entrées that the sea provides is the fish Hawaiians call mahi-mahi, the dolphinfish. Available in gourmet markets, it is often scorned by buyers who confuse it with the sea mammal called by the same name. Baked on a hibachi or in the oven with a seasoned sauce, mahi-mahi is a succulent and flavorful seafood served with rice.

A Caribbean diner's delight is a creature that lives in the familiar conch shell, called lambi. A giant snail with projecting bright yellow eyes, its flesh is tough and rubbery. Once it has been marinated, the meat is pounded with a wooden mallet. "He beat him like a lambi" is an island expression that attests to the violence with which lambi must be attacked if it is to be made edible.

Sea urchins are gobbled up like candy in the Caribbean and Mediterranean and in Japan and Chile. Even though great numbers of the animals live off the coasts of the United States, consumption of the prickly creatures is not common. A U.S. government bulletin on the subject suggests that the hostess who seeks novelties should serve "the orange seg-

*Sea cucumbers* are displayed on a wooden block next to a grouping of sea squirts prepared for sale in the port of Pusan, South Korea.

ments of the gonads like tangerines, arranged as a seafood cocktail with lemon juice." Caribbean housewives serve urchin reproductive organs in this way but prefer them sautéed in butter and blended with onions. Maybe the most unconventional treat from the sea is the violet, a bitter, iodine-filled ascidian that Mediterranean gourmets cut open and gobble down after seasoning it with a squeeze of lemon.

Algae may seem like food suitable only for snails that keep the sides of aquariums clean, but many recipes for the use of large algae are found in foreign cookbooks. Sea lettuce, *Ulva,* can be added to salads or chopped and cooked with zucchini and tomato sauce. A sticky candy is made from bladder kelp. Japanese cooks weave entire meals from the several varieties of kelp they eat. There may be more to eating kelp and sea cucumbers than a dietary treat: a relationship has been made between the fish diet of Orientals and a low incidence of heart disease. Overweight Westerners who shun sea creatures for a diet of meat and potatoes may gain better health as well as adding spice to their life from eating foods from the sea.

## The Gift of the Oyster

In France, as late as 1720, the wearing of pearls was forbidden to any but royalty as a measure of the esteem in which pearls were held. Although pearls were most valued from the fifteenth to nineteenth centuries, they appeared in ancient Egyptian tombs. Ruling classes in ancient Greece and Rome also treasured the jewels from the sea.

Pearls are formed by many molluscs that live in both fresh and salt water. The calcareous stones may be white, red, green, or black. Those pearls with the greatest beauty are formed by the oyster family, Aviculidae. If an irritant such as a grain of sand or a parasitic worm becomes lodged under the mollusc's mantle, the oyster deposits a secretion about the object and a pearl is born.

In 1891 a young Japanese noodle salesman conceived the idea of pearl culture. By 1920 the process had put an end to most searches for natural pearls. The jewel was now within the financial reach of the middle class. Pearls are induced to grow in an oyster by the insertion of a piece of shell or plastic into the mantle of the oyster. If the insertion is suc-

cessful, the tissue forms a pearl sack around the irritant. Nacre, the iridescent substance that lines the shells of many oysters and abalone, is then deposited to form a pearl. The oysters are held in baskets suspended from rafts for several years. The pearls are removed and spent shells are sold for the nacre lining—mother-of-pearl—which is used in the manufacture of buttons or in jewelry.

Today most pearl divers seek the oyster for the mother-of-pearl. The demand for this product has caused some oyster culturists to have as their prime business mother-of-pearl rather than pearls themselves.

Curiously, a mother-of-pearl farm was successfully worked in the early twentieth century, even before the Japanese oyster culture was successful. The Sudanese government started the farm that produced regular crops of 300 tons of pearl oysters from a bay in the Red Sea that normally yielded only 7 tons of oysters. When the price of mother-of-pearl fell after World War I, the farm was abandoned and its lessons forgotten. In 1957 a paper describing the farm was rediscovered and the Sudanese government, with the help of the United Nations, reestablished more than 100 privately owned "button" farms. Divers, who were depleting natural populations of oysters, are now trained farmers.

*Nestling in the hand of a pearl merchant (opposite) is a **perfect pearl**. Pearl divers usually work in tandem (above). The diver (below) pulls oysters from a reef in the Tuamotus.*

capital of the Western world. Coral from Tunisia, northern Africa, the Island of Tabarka, Corsica, and Sardinia, as well as that from Japan, was, and is today, purchased by Italian dealers. Most of the coral is channeled into the city of Torre de Greco near Naples, where hundreds of artisans polish the "stone" and work it into jewelry. Large branches of coral are sometimes left intact, just polished and mounted. These reddish coral "trees" sell for thousands of dollars, depending upon the number of branches.

In the past patrons or sponsors financed coral expeditions. The life of the coral fisherman was harsh and poor since most of the profit went to the patrons. After naked divers had depleted the red coral in shallow caves and cliffs, they turned to harvesting deeper with dredges. A cross-barred dredge, called the Cross of St. André, was pulled through the marine jungles. As the hard polyps were broken from the main reef, they fell into a

## Skeletal Jewels

Red coral has always been valued for its beauty. Coral pieces from the sixteenth century were so highly prized that they became a medium of exchange in financial dealings between Europeans and Asians. Beginning in the sixteenth century, Mediterranean men went out in boats in search of the precious coral which are really the nonliving skeletons of one specific species of coral animals. As reefs of red coral were located, they became family property, passed from father to son. Eventually men even fought wars over the right to take coral from the Mediterranean. The French and Italians staged a violent struggle that ended with the Italians' domination of the coral fisheries.

In the late eighteenth century all rivalries were calmed, and one city became the coral

60

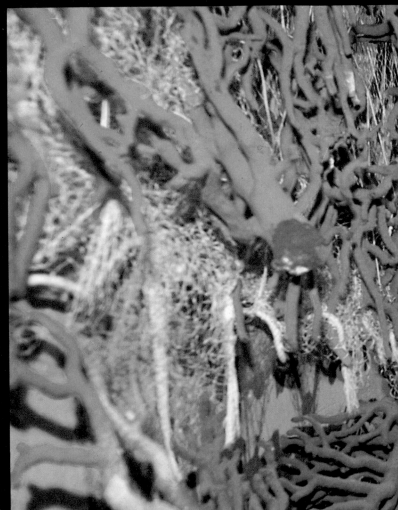

collecting net. Today in the Mediterranean the Cross would bring back nothing. The last existing coral trees are only to be found by daring deep divers in rare caves at depths of 300 to 400 feet. In a few years almost all precious red coral will be a souvenir of the past.

Coral fishing was not profitable in Japan until after 1830. Before that most red coral had to be presented to the shoguns, the regional rulers. Today, the Japanese practice the ancient techniques but sell their catch on the world market. They shun the dangerous life of their modern European contemporaries and do not dive for coral. They still seek out a reef, dredge, exhaust the coral, and then abandon the area, taking thousands of years of accumulation of coral branches in a very short time. Late in 1965 a rich bed of coral was discovered 300 miles northwest of Midway Island. The red coral was depleted by 1970. The dredging kills the living coral as well as other reef inhabitants.

Coral today is increasingly scarce, and scarcity means high price. In a bracelet with alternate, entwining circles of coral and gold, the price of adding a link of coral is almost as expensive as a gold one. Pinkish white coral, the most sought-after variety, sold for $300 per pound in the uncut state just a few years ago. Today a New York jeweler states, "We used to buy coral by the kilo; now we take—what we can get—by the carat."

To fill the demand, coral dust from the polishing is collected and molded into blocks for carving. The reconstituted coral sells for just half the cost of "real" coral.

*Coral* from a diver's collection basket (opposite) will be taken to land for cleaning. The branch on the left, polished and mounted, will bring over $500 on the retail market.

*Red coral branches,* worth thousands of dollars, line the walls of a diver's home (below). The coral has been cleaned but is still considered raw.

## Daring Divers

Le Corailleur is the nickname of a greedy and daring man whose romantic life belongs to the coral. He is one of the few Mediterranean coral divers left. These divers are eager to make fast money and to spend it even faster; but they are passionate about their profession and are infected with coral fever. They must, however, pay for their heroic status in their communities. Many show the effects of long years of diving too deep and for too long. They have atrophied legs and suffer from respiratory complaints. Each year several of them die when accidents or misjudgments keep them down too long.

One coral fisherman, who has been successful for many years, explains why he has not suffered accidents. He is more conservative than some of his peers. He says that when he tastes nitrogen on his tongue and begins to feel the effects of rapture of the deep, he immediately prepares to return to the surface even though it is at this time that divers invariably see one last, perfect specimen.

The modern coral fisherman is not a poor man at the mercy of a patron. Most own expensive, well-equipped boats. They have put to use all the equipment that modern technology affords. Echo sounders help them to locate new areas to fish. They dive with the finest and newest diving aids to supplement their considerable skill underwater. The typical diver carries a chipping hammer, a collection basket, and an inflatable marker buoy. When fully dressed and ready for work, the modern coral hunter carries over 140 pounds of gear and air tanks.

Divers work in tandem with another man. The partner waits on the boat for the 45 minutes the worker is below. The diver chips away at the coral, letting the pieces gently fall into the collecting bag. When his time underwater reaches its limit or his bag is filled, he inflates the buoy that is attached to the collection bag. He makes long decompression stops before climbing into the boat.

The coral-fishing season usually lasts six months of the year. Two to three kilos of coral are collected by a two-man team in a day, with each making two dives. As soon as the team returns to shore, they cure the coral so that it will maintain its color. The branches are soaked in clorox and water for about a half hour. The living coral is easy to peel away from the skeletons that are now ready to be sold to the Italian dealers. A coral diver can easily earn more money in a season than a business executive. But by having no concern for the conservation of red coral, these divers are ensuring the end of their occupation and way of life.

*A diver (top) guides his **precious coral** booty up from the sea. The coral diver (left) must use caution when breaking off the branches with the pick.*

*Red coral made into jewelry is the skeleton of the animal. The **living coral polyps** (opposite) construct the red "stone" and protrude to feed.*

## Marine Architects

Frank Lloyd Wright, the American architect, urged his students to examine the designs in nature, especially those in sea shells. He said that the housing of the sea, although lowly compared to the great edifices of man, had what human architecture often lacked—inspired form matched to complex function.

Man's attachment to shells, and his fascination with their beauty, surpasses his involvement with almost any other natural object. The first money used by primitive man actually was cowrie shells. Later, the Aztecs traded shells to the Spanish, who passed them as currency to African colonies with whom they had dealings. American Indians wove cowrie shells into money chains they referred to as wampum. Even today, purchase of a shell can be a judicious investment. A great spotted cowrie shell, of which only 18 are known to exist in the world, was offered for sale in late 1973 for $1750.

Shell motifs are found in art throughout the world. Religions and folktales abound with stories of the power of the shell. Aphrodite,

*Black coral (below) is prized by many cultures, even having a religious significance for Moslems. A diver (left) saws the coral branches. Another (top) returns them to the surface vessel.*

the Greek goddess of love and beauty, arose from a scallop shell. The same fable is related about the birth of Quetzalcoatl, the Mayan god of goodness. Sudanese natives today wear the cowrie shell as a symbol of fertility.

The popularity of shell collecting has stimulated the opening of hundreds of shell shops around the world, especially concentrated in tourist and resort areas near the sea. Fifteen such shops operate in Honolulu alone. Most of the shells that they offer for sale are common. They are taken by the beachcombers. Many of the shells that form a valuable inventory for the shops are collected by divers. Collecting marine life for only their shells must surely be condemned. A diving biologist recently visited some South Pacific islands, intending to photograph some of the more interesting shelled animals. He found none. Islanders explained that he would find good shelling areas no closer than a day's boat ride from any local airport. All other areas had been scoured by shell collectors who had taken living animals as well.

Most criticism of shell-collecting divers has centered around the destruction that they have allegedly caused on the Great Barrier Reef in Australia. Royal triton shells are in great demand because of their beauty and are taken in large numbers from the Australian reefs. Recently there has been a proliferation of the crown-of-thorns starfish, one of whose main predators is the triton snail. Some feel that overpopulation of this starfish, which may be contributing to destruction of the reefs, is due in part to diminishing numbers of its predator by diving shell collectors. (At the moment scientific evidence does not support any of these claims.)

*Admiration for the inspired beauty of design in many **shells** (right) has led to reef devastation by divers, who take every shelled animal in sight, in the hope of selling them to collectors.*

# Chapter VI. The Clever Predator

Before the time of hook, harpoon, and fleets of trawlers, we fished like the other land animals—by grabbing our prey out of the water with our hands. This is a practice still used in some parts of the world to catch lethargic fish. Clams and oysters were the easiest animals to be caught without the use of elaborate gear and were probably man's first seafood. Great mounds of oyster shells that accumulated thousands of years ago in northern Europe attest to the popularity shellfish had for our ancestors.

Simple hooks were invented, probably in imitation of the curved claws that helped bears snatch fast-swimming prey from freshwater streams. The hooks were made from

---

**"Simple fishing methods did not often allow the clever predator to outsmart himself and eliminate his source of food by overfishing."**

---

stone or sharp bones. The first nets may have evolved from the observation that fish seek shelter in reeds and kelp beds and are easy to catch when they become entangled there.

Until the advent of mechanized boats and gear, we were just another predator, competing with the other carnivores for food from the sea. Our advantage over our prey was not great; that is still the case today in a few societies. Simple fishing methods very often involved imagination, ingenuity, and an enormous amount of experience and behavioral knowledge about marine creatures. But they did not often allow the clever predator to outsmart himself and eliminate his source of food by overfishing. Small groups of people, huddled together on a beach or living a roving existence on the sea like the

Asians who settled Polynesia by constantly pushing their boats toward the rising sun, could not deplete the food riches in the sea. The earth's population was small. Man's fishing and food needs were more modest in scale. For example, the precursor of the trawl net was a scoop formed from nets strung between poles. One man operated the net and was able to catch many more fish than with hook alone. Even so, the numbers of fish he could take were miniscule compared to the modern trawl net. We were hunters but we only hunted to satisfy the needs of our families. From the time we first tasted seafood through all the primitive societies up until the advent of the steam engine, our fishing weapons did not pose great threats to the fish of the sea.

Prior to the eighteenth century, few marine animals were overharvested from simple food needs. The murex shellfish was depleted from the eastern Mediterranean by the Phoenicians, but these were cleaned out for the valuable murex dye. Food needs alone would never have been so great as to cause the depletion of an entire animal population.

Every predation remained at a human scale. Probably the first time man was truly able to overpower the ocean's animals was with the invention of the harpoon gun in 1860. By 1880, when its use was generalized throughout the whaling industry, man's war against the living resources of the sea began in earnest and continues to this day with an intensity that depletes a new fishing ground within 10 years.

*A native fishing alone with simple gear can take enough fish only for a few days. For centuries, the sea's living resources were not overly exploited. The sea did not feel the stress of man's predation.*

## Old-Fashioned Lures

A complete collection of so-called primitive fishing gear would fill many rooms with fascinating testimony to early man's understanding of fish behavior. Obviously a large body of knowledge of marine-life cycles was gained long before we coined the terms *marine biologist* and *animal behavior*.

None of the tools of fishing, in any time, are of use without an understanding of where and when fish will be attracted to them. Aside from luck, luring the fish to the bait was, and is, one of the most important chores facing a fisherman. Fishing societies that could not depend upon electronics and advanced gear developed this art to a high degree and serve to illustrate that bait is more than a fat worm on the end of a hook.

Fish are highly sensitive to odors. Fishermen on the Upper Rhine River still put female salmon in their traps during spawning season to lure the male to the trap. Some strong-smelling substances have been used to attract fish since earliest times. Favorites are anise, musk, heron's oil, and castor.

Certain species of fish that have a highly developed sense of territory attack an intruder of the same species if one invades its boundaries. Japanese fishermen tie a living ayu to lines near unbaited hooks. Another ayu is hooked when it attacks the intruder.

The fishermen of Oceania know that sharks are as curious as cats. Vibrations in the water will draw sharks from great distances. The natives beat the surface of the water with coconut shell rattles. The noise and disruption in the water draws sharks to the surface where they are caught with rope loops.

Hundreds of years ago it was noticed that some small fish were attracted to light on a dark night. Europeans held burning torches on the beach and stabbed the assembled fish with tridents. Boats equipped with lamps are still used to draw sardines from the depths to surface nets in the Mediterranean.

Bait is successful only if it attracts a fish to a hook or to a trap. At first the selection of suitable materials to lure fish was made by trial and error but probably based on logic. A fish which had been observed eating fish eggs might be drawn to them on a hook.

Some marine animals ignore exotic odors and members of the opposite sex most of the year. Shy animals try to hide. When they find a suitable crevice or cave, they settle down. Lobster traps and octopus jars are based on this trait. Trap effectiveness is often enhanced by bait. The fisherman who understands what draws a lobster to a pot, for example, is more apt to feed his family than one unfamiliar with such subtleties.

*An aborigine pulls a **giant beach worm,** Onuphis teres, from the sand (opposite). It will be eaten raw.*

***Octopus jars** (right) are effective because the animal needs a hiding place. The octopus first checks out the suitability of the trap. Since it seems appropriate, he crawls in. Later, fishermen haul up the jar.*

# Animal Assistants

Dogs are the most common animal man has trained to help him capture food. Rarely, though, has the dog been helpful in fishing. Many breeds swim, but only the Portuguese water dog is adapted to retrieve fish as hunting dogs bring back waterfowl. Natives in northern Japan have succeeded in training dogs to work in packs in shallow water. They move toward shore, frightening the fish into nets. Fish heads are saved for the dogs as a reward.

Any animal whose natural habitat is the water is candidate to be a companion to the fisherman. The otter is such an animal. Marco Polo brought back stories of Chinese fishermen using freshwater otters as assistants in the Yangtze River. Their use was also popular in India. English sportsmen picked up the idea as a hunting fad in the eighteenth century, importing trained otters from Asia to use in trout fishing.

The animals were muzzled so that they wouldn't eat the fish as they chased them into nets, like sheep dogs herding their flocks up a hillside. The otters remained with their masters for their lifetime—up to 15 years.

About the same time that the royal sport of falconry developed, another bird was first trained to catch fish. Cormorants have been used in river fishing in Japan since 813 A.D. They are taken captive when only a few months old and undergo training sessions four or five times a day until they are accustomed to their masters. Just like the falcon, they dive for their prey on command. A string around the throat prevents them from swallowing all but the smallest fish, which serve as their food. Efficient birds can catch up to a hundred fish in an hour.

For more than a thousand years dolphins have helped Moorish fishermen by frighten-

*Oriental fishermen* (above) have used cormorants to retrieve fish for a thousand years. Some Indo-Chinese (opposite) catch fish aided by otters.

ing schools of mullets into their nets, but only one fish has been used directly for capturing other marine animals. The remora, or suckfish, is used as an actual accessory to fishing.

Remoras have a large sucker that has evolved as a spectacular restructuring of the dorsal fin. Fishermen in diverse parts of the world use the sucker of the remora as a living fish hook. The remoras are strung on lines and when a turtle, or even a shark, is sighted, the little fish are tossed in the direction of the prey. If they attach to the passing animal, they are pulled back to the boat by a line looped around their bodies in front of the tail fin. Amazingly, the remoras are strong enough to withstand the tug-of-war between fisherman and fish.

*Reef Islanders (above and opposite, top) pull **scoop nets** through shallow water to ensnare small fish.*

*__Turkana fishermen__ (opposite) in northern Kenya prepare to set semipermanent beach nets.*

## Godly Quotas

Societies that depended on fish as food and whose fishermen worked singly could not seriously deplete fish stocks in their waters. Even so, they recognized that overfishing could eventually affect their food supply and had to be avoided. Understanding that preserving the source of food was good strategy, they very spontaneously invented the first laws of ecology.

Primitive societies devised ways to protect fish populations, and incorporated them into religious beliefs. Many societies thought of fish as man's brother hiding in a different body. The first fish caught or a drop of the fisherman's blood was returned to the sea as atonement for the killing of a fellow creature.

Only the Egyptians, in the earliest times of their history, shunned the ocean. Seafood was prohibited and only the most sacrilegious would eat it. Priests never touched anything that had come from the sea. Naturally Egyptian fishermen made no impact on the fish populations in the Mediterranean.

Laws regulating fish catches were god-given in most primitive societies. To disobey them was to risk the wrath of the sea gods. The rules were not lightly ignored and the fish population not often diminished.

South American Indian religions still prohibit the taking of fish during the spawning season and dictate that young fish be tossed back. The number of fish taken must not exceed the amount that can be eaten in one day. Fish left on the beach to rot are an insult to the ghosts. Poor fishing, famine, illness, and death will soon follow.

Modern fishing gear has contributed to the loss of old ways and traditions that respected the creatures of the sea. A purchaser of native-made nets in Vietnam, for example, must pay a tax to buy a sacrifice to the sea goddess. The purveyors of imported, machine-made nets command no such homage. The implication is that the modern equipment is so efficient that it does not require outside, godly assistance. Thus allegiance to the old rules has been diminished.

Modern fishermen find it easier to disobey international fishing quotas than their ancestors did to defy the powers of their gods. Irreverence has led to a loss of appreciation for the fragile bounty of the sea.

# Chapter VII. The Food Myth

The immensity of the ocean inspires trust. We tend to think of the sea as having an infinite ability to absorb our trash and sewage and an unrestricted power to give food and natural resources. But like all old friends, she too has her limits, and science is finding such limits to be pretty narrow.

Great demands have been placed on the ocean's supply of fish. With military precision, some nations sweep across the seas, taking every living thing. When criticized, they answer that they must feed their citizens. But there are too many people to feed.

The population controversy was first sparked in the late eighteenth century by Thomas Malthus. Speaking to a world inhabited by a much smaller population than that of today, he said that world population could be expected to increase geometrically

---

**"The sea can't provide food for the billions who will sit down to dinner in the year 2000."**

---

while the food supply could only develop arithmetically. Thus, at some point, the population would outstrip the capacity of the earth to feed it. Since this idea was first proposed, scientific agriculture has expanded food supplies to a much greater degree than Malthus foresaw, and by savagely plundering all kinds of natural resources, mankind was able to forget Malthus temporarily. Stuart Mill further prophesied that the population explosion and our materialistic civilization would lead to disaster, including food shortages. The quality of life was at stake. Stuart Mill was rediscovered as a result of the concern for the environment that stirred the 1960s. Malthus's ideas also gained a new, widespread audience.

However, fresh warnings of imminent world famine were dismissed by many with the answer that our dependable sea would provide: it was only a matter of time before technology would succeed in extracting packets of sea energy to feed all of us.

There is no doubt that the ocean could be more productive than it is at present, but certainly not by the improvement of fishing methods. Fishing, however modern, is nothing else than hunting was for primitive man. It consists of eating up our heritage, instead of cashing dividends from our estate. Fishing to feed the world is as naive as trying to feed billions by hunting wildlife. In the sea, as on land, comprehensive farming is the only answer. Advanced fishing gear, bigger fleets of modern vessels, and expansion of fishing into new areas can hardly maintain the world fish catch at its present level. Even if it could double it for a short time, by the year 2000 the sea will only supply about 8 percent of the energy requirements of the 6 billion people who will be sitting down to dinner at the end of this century.

Many fish populations are already being reduced beyond their ability to reproduce. Atlantic salmon, herring, certain whales—the list goes on—may have already suffered irreversible damage. It is foolish and irresponsible to continue to make such demands on the sea. If we manage our fishing and replace what we take by farming, we can trust the sea to continue to provide. But she can serve only a certain number of people. We cannot expect, like children, to take forever, even from the most loving of parents, without returning the gift and curbing our wants.

*When entire **schools of fish** are taken hourly by factory ships, the sea's bounty is quickly diminished.*

# Fish Factories

The leaders in the fish business have traditionally been the Japanese. They have recently slipped slightly behind, under the massive onslaught on the sea by the Russians, but they still hold their own as one of the world's most powerful fishing nations.

Smaller fishing operations and boats are being driven out of business in Japan each year. Fewer, but larger, vessels desert the polluted coastal waters off Japan every season to head out over the global seas, in search of new fishing grounds. Japanese fishermen take over 9 million metric tons of fish each year. Virtually every living resource from the sea is taken by their boats.

The most popular catch is still the tuna. The development of long-line fishing, in which baited hooks are strung from miles of horizontal lines, enables Japanese vessels to take 60 percent of the world's catch in tuna. Their boats dominate the Pacific and are often in the Caribbean. In 1957 the waters of the Atlantic were entered by Japanese boats for the first time. The tuna catch is already down, indicating overexploitation. An identical situation has developed in the Indian Ocean, where over 200 Japanese boats continually fish for a diminishing number of tuna.

To help offset the cost of fishing far from their homeland and to improve relations with coastal nations, the Japanese have entered into joint venture agreements with many countries. They fish within other's territorial seas in exchange for the business they generate on foreign shores. They purchase supplies, storage facilities, and onshore crew accommodations in coastal nations all over the world, as they fish foreign waters.

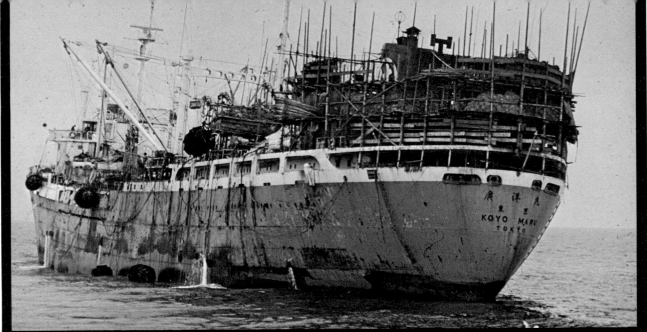

*Alaskan king crab* are taken by the thousands by large Japanese vessels. The Koyo Maru (above) is used to both catch and process crab. On deck (opposite and below) the legs are removed. Onboard processing enables the vessel to forage far from home for long periods of time.

The Russians also have a far-flung fishing operation made possible by an armada of vessels that resembles a naval operation in its methods. Administrators direct fishing activities in each of the major seas like fleet commanders maneuvering their forces in battle. As many as 300 ships will travel in massive flotillas accompanied by factory ships and transport vessels.

Russians waste nothing from the sea. Huge factory ships begin the processing just as soon as a catch is taken onboard. One such ship, the *Professor Baranov*, is 543 feet long. It is able to salt 200 tons of herring, process 150 tons of fish into meal, filet and freeze 100 tons of bottom fish, and manufacture 5 tons of fish oil, 20 tons of ice, and 100 tons of distilled water—all in one day. The cost of a Soviet invasion of the sea is absorbed by the government. A fishing fleet with such a high subsidy from national funds certainly puts other fishing nations—and the fish— at a distinct disadvantage.

# Freedom to Fish?

Historically, the seas belonged to no one nation. Mere navigation rules evolved to avoid collisions between ships of different flags using the ocean as a highway. For purposes of navigation only, it was established that the open sea belonged to all nations, but for anything else it was no man's land. Early in the eighteenth century, the area within the artillery range of a coastal state, usually about three miles out from shore, was declared the property of the coastal state. Regulations governing the harvesting of ocean resources, particularly fish, were not necessary as long as countries fished near their own shores.

Today's technology enables successful fishing nations to travel the world over in search of bigger and better catches. This has prompted many countries to extend their territorial limits farther seaward. Peru and Ecuador, among others, claim 200 miles as their territorial sea. Such claims have caused turmoil among nations that fish close to foreign shores. By the end of 1972 Ecuador had captured over 80 U.S. tuna boats for fishing within her waters. Most recently, clashes between Iceland and Great Britain over fishing rights in the North Atlantic have been in the headlines. The British navy had to be summoned to protect her trawlers that were fishing within Iceland's 50-mile sea. England honors only a 12-mile limit and feels that its boats have the right to fish within the same distance from Iceland's shores. Iceland, on the other hand, believes that it has an obligation to protect the livelihood of her fishermen by ensuring that foreign fleets do not deplete stocks. The dispute has been taken to the United Nations.

*A **trawl net** surfaces with over 30,000 pounds of fish. It will be hoisted on board and then set out to be pulled behind the trawler again.*

Several regulatory agencies have been formed in attempts to protect certain species from extinction. The International Pacific Fur Seal Commission and the International Pacific Halibut Commission are perhaps the two agencies that have met with some success in enforcing their regulations. Through prudent management, each has restored an overexploited and dwindling resource to the extent that it can now be harvested without further endangering its populations.

In general, other commissions have met with little success, if not spectacular failure. However, their continued existence is of extreme importance to the future of fishing. Commissions such as the International North Pacific Fisheries Commission and the International Commission of North American Fisheries sponsor important research and assemble data vital to the future establishment of regulations limiting the catch. This is done by restricting the number of boats fishing a certain species, setting the type of gear that can be used and by establishing an annual catch quota for a certain fish. All such regulations are aimed at producing a level of fishing effort that will allow the greatest number of fish to be taken without depleting the breeding populations below a productive level. This point is called maximum sustainable yield and is the ideal.

Fishery commissions generally fall short in their ability to enforce regulations. Protection of living resources from continued overexploitation will require herculean efforts and a spirit of international cooperation. The United Nations and many other international bodies have taken up the challenge. Living resources were declared the common property of mankind. It is in the world's vital interest to give them proper management and protection, but such resolutions have still to be practically implemented.

## Racing to Destruction

In 1970 the world catch of fish, including molluscs and crustaceans, rose to a record high of slightly more than 68 million tons. In 1948 the landing was only 19.6 million tons. This more-than-threefold increase in slightly over 20 years can be attributed to advances in fishery technology. Even though more sophisticated gear is in operation, the peak catch of 1970 has not been matched since. Overfishing has taken its toll.

The Japanese and Russians are perhaps the two most industrialized fishing nations in the world. In 1970 Japan, landing 9.3 million metric tons, was a leading fishing nation, second only to Peru. The Soviets took 7.3 million metric tons from the sea in the same year. The United States ranked a distant sixth place, landing only 3 million tons.

Japan and Russia fish areas to their limit, then move on. This method, called pulse fishing, leaves fishermen who are restricted to coastal waters with depleted stocks from which to nurse a living. In 1965 large Russian fleets moved onto the Georges Bank off the northeast coast of the United States and took tremendous amounts of haddock. This is a species of considerable value to American and Canadian fishermen. By the end of 1967 the Russians, disregarding attempts by the International Commission for the Northwest Atlantic Fisheries to regulate the haddock catch, had almost wiped out the fish from those waters. To this day, the fishery has not recovered. Fishery scientists have estimated that the 1963 year class of haddock, largest on record, could have supported a U.S.-Canadian fishery for 10 years.

The Japanese have been similarly irresponsible. They have shown little interest in conservation. Their fisheries research lies solely in the development and expansion of

catches. Conservation is ignored. The attitudes of the Japanese toward fisheries management, when they sit around an international conference table, is aptly illustrated by the following remark by a leading Japanese fishery biologist to the International North Pacific Fisheries Commission some years ago: "It appears that fishery biology should not restrict itself to the question of conservation, which is primarily concerned

80

with the means to protect what is now being exploited. More attention should be paid to the development of fisheries and the exploitation of new resources. Fishery biology should not be a conservation science." This approach to fisheries management has made international bargaining difficult.

In fact, today's game is to overfish and deplete somebody else's backyard. Unless the nations of the world can curb their greed, it is conceivable that by 1980 there will be no healthy fish stocks left in the oceans. Only urgent and close cooperation between all nations in matters of resource management can prevent the ultimate destruction of the fishery resources of the entire world.

*Buyers and sellers haggle over the price of tuna at a Tokyo auction. Most of the tuna will go to local markets and restaurants for sashimi, raw-fish appetizers, or any number of dishes.*

# Fishing Oceanographers

Locating fish in the ocean can be an incredibly difficult task. Before the advent of advanced technology, old-timers had their tricks for finding fish. They watched for terns and gulls circling an area as an indication that the birds were feeding on bait pushed to the surface by the activity of a school of large predators such as tuna. For the most part, however, locating the catch was based on a long tradition of observations, transmitted from captain to captain; and as fish habits vary according to such factors as temperature and salinity, which were unknown, luck played an important role. An experienced captain's good eye scanning the blank sea was probably the best catch locating asset a boat could have.

Today electronics and space technology are put to use as fish finders. The echo sounder

*Small fishing boats* (above) in Kanto Choshi, Japan, are rapidly losing out to large fleets equipped with efficient fish-finding gear.

was originally developed as an aid to navigation. The nature of the bottom was revealed by ultrasonic beams bounced back to the ship. Since schooling fish also showed up on the screen, fishermen soon saw the use for the echo sounder in their business. Improvements in design now enable the scanner to relay information so detailed that the fisherman can ascertain the type of fish schooling beneath and around his boats. If there is no market for the species, time need not be spent in catching it.

Echo-sounding equipment aboard two scout ships is a critical part of a herring-locating system that is so successful that its developers have become national heroes in Iceland. Twenty years ago schools of herring were located by sight when they came near the surface. Mysteriously the behavior of the fish changed; the schools stopped making surface appearances. Since the herring make long spawning and feeding migrations, the Icelandic fishermen were spending over half the eight-month fishing season in profitless searches. The new system sends a research boat out to take temperature, current, and other hydrographic data prior to the opening of the season. Scientists make predictions about where the herring will appear in the coming weeks and months. Scout ships with echo sounders are sent to define precisely the position of major schools. Only then does the fleet set out. Instead of spending time in searching for their prey, they continuously fish all eight months of the season.

Sensitive cameras on high-flying planes and satellites can record the presence of schooling fish by the disturbance they make as they swim through the bioluminescent glow of plankton. Fish also give away their positions to ultrasensitive microphones. The clicks that crabs make and the sounds of communication that some fish emit can be picked up from as far as 15 miles away. Dolphins squeak, whales sing, and haddock and cod make low mutterings. Microphones working with computers programmed to identify the exact species of schooling fish could be part of the payload of far-ranging unmanned submersibles.

Fishermen may soon find out that they, themselves, are obsolete. An automatic system, based on the fact that fish are drawn to the positive pole of an electrode like iron filings to a magnet, has been developed. It would be possible to direct the fish caught in the electric fields, herd them into small troughs, and pump them on board a floating platform, where they are processed.

*Echo sounders make the location of large **schools of fish** (below) an easy task. Days spent searching out the catch are eliminated.*

## Fisherman or Industrialist?

The fishing industry is at a troubling cross-roads. In one direction lie the old values—free enterprise, individualism, private ownership, and a severely limited ability to compete with foreign fishing fleets. In the other direction is increased government intervention to provide funds for expensive, but competitive, factory fleets. The first line respects the personal relationship between the fisher-

man and the sea and includes a faint possibility of protecting what can still be saved. But it certainly puts a country at a loss in the international race for short-term production at all costs.

Steeped in tradition, fishing in most of the Western countries is one of the oldest arts. Most boats are small and old; they are repaired rather than replaced with large ships with more modern gear because the cost of such ships is prohibitive to private owners.

Most fishermen oppose the development of government-owned or subsidized fleets like those of the Soviets. The fisherman with a small operation knows that a national fishing fleet could compete with the foreign ones they see taking huge catches from waters that they have always considered their own private ponds. But they also know that factory ships, no matter which country's flag they fly, will further reduce the catches and profits of small competitors. If you wander into a small New England village and question assembled fishermen about what they see as the solution to America's fishing problems, most will urge the extension of territorial waters out to 200 miles. The U.S. government can't comply with this request without upsetting tuna fishermen who lobby in Washington for protection for their boats inside the 200-mile limits imposed by some South American nations.

So far, most governments have tried to assist the fishermen, but in less controversial ways. Low-interest loans are available for repairing and replacing boats. Government-sponsored research seeks new fishing grounds and makes information about them available.

With the exception of the Swiss Nestle Company, most of the huge corporations of the Western world that pack and distribute fish products do not operate their own modern fleets because it is cheaper to buy fish directly from foreign fisheries than to invest their funds in vessels.

As an example, $1 billion in fish imports entered the United States in 1972. Only $139 million was exported. Significantly, 44 percent of the U.S. catch was "trash fish," destined to become fish meal or cat and dog food. Because the U.S. fishing fleet does not include many refrigerated ships, most boats cannot range far from shore to take the species that are in popular demand.

An additional point of view needs mentioning. In North America as well as in Europe, the voice of conservation poses the question: Can the ocean support massive fish takes? What is the morality that urges us to take as many fish as we can—because if we don't, the Russians or the Japanese will?

*The **trawler** Swan comes home to Monterey, California. Boats of this size aren't capable of the vast sweeps made by big, mechanized factory ships.*

85

## El Niño and the Anchovy

Russian factory ships and Japanese fleets scour the world's oceans, taking massive, catches of many varieties of fish. Peru's fishermen concentrate on one fish—the anchovy—and fish only within 200 miles of shore. Even so, the world's largest commercial catch, by weight, is Peruvian.

A few years ago, Peru hardly rated on a list of major fishing nations. The anchovy industry did not begin in earnest until 1957. Easy success led hundreds of boats into the field. Subsequently, dozens of fish meal factories were constructed to process the catch. In 1970, $340 million in foreign money entered Peru as a direct result of the anchovy industry.

Coastal Peruvian waters are abundant in food for the anchovy. Upwelling supplies nutrients to support plentiful plankton growth in the cold waters pulled northward by the offshore Humboldt Current.

Every few years a warm current dips down from the equator to displace the Humboldt. It is called El Niño ("The Child") because it often makes its appearence near the Christmas season. But El Niño does not bring joy. The warm current interrupts upwelling, plankton growth decreases, and the life of

*A few members of the massive **Peruvian anchovy fleet** tie up (above left) near a fish meal plant.*

***Anchovies*** *are pumped on board (above). The catch has diminished due to overfishing.*

***Guano birds*** *nest (below) in one of hundreds of rookeries off the coast of Peru. Reduction of the anchovy population has had a detrimental effect on the birds. Competition with man for the diminishing fish population has caused many of the birds to die of starvation or to desert the area.*

the anchovy becomes a chaotic search for diminishing food supplies. Their schools disperse as they are further reduced by an influx of predators—yellowfin tuna and hammerhead sharks—that move in on the warm stream. The air becomes foul with the smell of dying fish and "guano birds" that depend on the anchovy for survival. Fishermen come home with empty boats, tarred black from the decay in the water.

The past two El Niño situations, in 1965 and 1972, had particularly extreme effects on the anchovy. Usually the fish population quickly recovers from the devastation. Fishermen reported good catches from 1965 through 1971. Then, in the spring of 1972, an abrupt drop in the anchovy catch occurred. By the end of the season, only one-quarter of the number of fish taken the previous season had been landed. El Niño had come but the fishermen had to take their share of the blame too: they had landed in excess of 2 million tons of anchovies the previous year over what had been recommended by fisheries biologists. The standing stock (overall population) of the anchovy is now estimated at 2 million metric tons, a reduction from 20 million tons in 1971.

The guano bird population has been similarly affected. Every El Niño reduces their numbers. Adults migrate to new food supplies as the anchovies die. Immature birds and nestlings starve. Even so, their return to normal population levels ordinarily takes only a short time. However, after El Niño in 1965 the birds did not return; their population now stands at 4.3 million, down from a 1957 high of 27 million.

Both the birds, whose droppings are sold for fertilizer, and the fish are important economic factors in Peru. Their disappearance would be a financial disaster. More than that, the loss of the anchovy as a source of food is unsettling at a time of protein shortage.

## Not the Only Fishes in the Sea

Many kinds of crustaceans and molluscs are "fished" in economically important industries. In the United States alone, the catch of shellfish, including squid, amounts to nearly 5 billion pounds, with a market value of over $640 million annually.

Along the east coast of the United States and Canada, the Atlantic lobster supports a big business. Landings of northern lobsters in the United States in 1972 brought $36 million at the market. Until recently, lobsters were so common along the New England coast that they could be caught with the bare hand at low tide. Today, however, these crustaceans are so scarce that their retail price has soared above that of any other seafood taken from the Atlantic.

Another group of crustaceans commonly called lobsters differs from the true lobsters in having no claws. They are members of the family *Panularidae* and are sometimes called spiny lobsters. These crustaceans constitute a worldwide market even larger than that of the true lobster and are found in subtropical and temperate waters. The major areas of spiny lobster production are south and southwest of Africa, the reefs off Australia and New Zealand and the Caribbean. Quite abundant 10 years ago in California and the Mediterranean, they have

*Maine* **lobster pots** *(above) await placement. Netting funnels lead lobsters to the bait and imprison them in a chamber called the parlor.*

**Atlantic lobster,** *true lobster (below left), have been sorted for market.* **Spiny lobster** *(below right), found in temperate waters, are not true lobster; they lack claws.*

now become very rare in these areas. The U.S. is the largest spiny lobster consumer, paying the highest prices for cold-water tails; France is second in consumption.

Fewer lobsters in shallow-water pots have sent the fishermen farther offshore. Instead of using pots, they dredge the bottom with trawl nets. Great numbers of the expensive catch are crushed in the process, as they are hauled aboard from depths up to 2000 feet. Increased consumption and overfishing, as well as pollution, are threatening lobster resources to the point that this tasty seafood soon might not appear on any restaurant menu for any price.

Other crustaceans of commercial importance are crabs and shrimp. The waters off Japan, Alaska, and Chile support a large industry based on the king crab. In the early 1960s it became apparent that international regulations were necessary to conserve the Alaskan king crab stocks from overharvesting. Catch quotas and gear regulations were agreed upon and these temporarily halted further expansion in the crab field. Scientists close to the problem indicate that 1970 regulations were very successful in reducing exploitation. The 1971 landings in Alaska alone were 70.4 million pounds, valued at $24.7 million, an increase of over 35 percent by volume. Perhaps the Alaskan king crab industry is one in which negotiations and regulations were implemented before the resource went too far down the road to oblivion.

In the early 1850s, an abalone fishery was established in California by emigrant Chinese nationals. The present fishery is centered in the Santa Barbara-Morro Bay regions and has been considerably restricted in the last decade. Government regulations on minimum size of the catch and depth at which the molluscs can be taken have helped to prevent total depletion of the stock.

*Traditional **Japanese diving women (ama)** are called, as a group, funando. They rest (above) after filling their baskets with abalone. **A modern abalone diver** (below) wrenches a shellfish from its undersea home. Because of overharvesting, the surviving abalone are found only in deep water.*

# Chicken Feed

If you had an egg for breakfast, you've eaten seafood today. This has been a fairly accurate statement since the development of fish meal as food for cattle and chicken. Animal food is made from "trash fish"—those species that are not popularly accepted for human consumption either because of traditional preferences or because their small size makes processing them an expensive business. These less-desirable species are often taken by trawlers seeking other varieties. In the past the unmarketable fish were tossed overboard. Since most did not survive the ordeal, considerable waste resulted. When the market for fish meal was developed, fleets began efforts to take trash fish. Today they comprise a third, by weight, of all fish caught. The process of turning sardines, anchovies, menhaden, and other small fish into chicken feed begins with cooking. Water and oil are extracted, leaving a powdery substance high in protein. Removal of the liquids from the fish mash has two important consequences. The weight, and thus the shipping cost, is reduced and spoilage is eliminated.

A similar mash has been developed for direct human consumption. Called FPC (fish protein concentrate), it has exciting possibilities for increasing the world's available protein. Unlike fresh fish in all respects, it is an odorless, flavorless substance, making an ideal additive for bread, pasta, cookies, and sauces.

FPC has not had an easy time. The American Food and Drug Administration forbade its consumption for "aesthetic" reasons. Since the entire fish—eyes, entrails, and scales—are used in the manufacture, it was felt that the buyer would be offended by FPC. In a bitter dispute in which it was pointed out that oysters are gobbled whole, even without being cooked, the government relented and allowed FPC to be distributed.

*The trash fish industry is highly mechanized. **A lift pump** (below) unloads the catch for processing.*

*Rejects of a **trawl catch** (right), these animals are now used for marine protein concentrates.*

Blades cut through **underwater kelp forests** (below right) and transfer the kelp to the **harvesting barge** (above). *A* **diver** (below) emerges from an ocean vegetable patch. The **kelp** (top right) is not damaged by the cutting; it recovers in a few months.

# Seaweed Succulents

Much has been made of the fact that ocean ecosystems, rich in plant life, support great populations of fish and other animals. This is, of course, a fact. It is also true that the closer to plants in the pyramid of life man seeks for his source of food, the more food will be available to him. So why do we not harvest great quantities of plants from ocean fields as we do from those on land? Primarily because the majority of the ocean's plants are one-celled. At the present stage of technology, it is not economically possible for our machines to imitate the baleen whale and filter tons of water to extract microscopic organisms. Even if far-ranging filtering pumps were devised, most of the ocean harvest could not serve as human food. The majority of plants in the "algae soup" are encapsulated by indigestible coverings of cellulose, silica (the main ingredient of glass), or calcareous plates.

The only sea plants that are of use as food to man are those that grow in fixed locations —seaweeds. It may be difficult to imagine that the evil-smelling kelp that washes up on the shore could be of much use beyond supporting colonies of flies but, properly processed, these large algae serve as important sources of food, fertilizer, and chemicals.

Only the Japanese eat great quantities of seaweed. One of their favorites is nori, dried laver, that is sold in flat sheets that can, among other things, be toasted and crumpled into soup to become an ocean crouton.

Forests of the giant kelp *Macrocystis* grow along the coasts of California, Brittany, and the southern coasts of South America. Harvested and processed, they prevent crystals from forming in ice cream and give toothpaste and paint a creamy texture. Algin, from kelp, maintains the foamy head on beer. Extracts from brown kelp are found in in over 300 products.

Commercial kelp operations rely on natural beds for raw material. The giant kelp recovers rapidly from harvesting; it grows at the rate of one to two feet in a single day. Strands and streamers several hundred feet long are cut to about three feet beneath the water by equipment that simultaneously carries the harvest on board barges. Since the reproductive parts of the plants are not destroyed, the same field can be cut again in four or five months. Cutting the crop may even contribute to kelp growth by allowing greater amounts of sunlight to reach new growth.

*Seaweed is draped over **drying racks** (below) as the first step in the processing of the algae for consumption in Japan. It is then gathered and packaged.*

## Modern Fishing

At the beginning of this decade, the living animal resources of the world's oceans were being hunted by 1.5 million fishing vessels and supporting ships based in every major and minor nation. These vessels range in size and complexity from a south sea islander's dugout to a 715-foot whale factory ship.

The design of a fishing craft is determined by the species of fish it will be hunting and the type of gear proven best for catching that fish. The most common commercial fishing vessel is the trawler. Virtually all fishing nations use them. They are named for the bag-like net they tow. The mouth of the net is held open by two heavy doors, called otter boards, that are forced apart by the water pushing against them. Otter trawls are very successful in taking groundfish like halibut, flounder, and cod; midwater trawls mainly catch hake, herring, and other species that do not live on or near the bottom. There are two types of vessels that carry these nets: side and stern trawlers. The former get their name from the manner in which the net is handled. It is set, towed, and hauled aboard over the side of the vessel. In many countries the side trawler is being replaced by the more-

modern stern trawler. These larger vessels have a stern ramp, or chute, that the net slides down as it is being placed in the water. After fishing an area, the net is brought back through the stern with a power block. Small stern trawlers, under 200 feet, usually lack a stern ramp but have a low, wide aft deck onto which the net is hauled.

Seining is another common method of catching fish. American fishermen like to use a purse seine, a large net set in a circle around a school of fish. The top of the net floats on the surface while the bottom is drawn together around a school of fish like an old-fashioned pocketbook. This technique is very successful in catching schools that inhabit surface waters. Tremendous amounts of menhaden and anchovies are taken annually by commercial purse seiners working coastal waters.

The boats used for purse seining are characterized by a wide, flat fishing deck aft and the wheelhouse forward. When the vessel is rigged for seining, the net is piled high on the stern and a seine skiff, used to string out the net, sits on top. Small purse seiners, 40 to 100 feet long, are used by fishermen on the Pacific coast of the United States to catch salmon, as the fish migrate to fresh water.

A third group of vessels also uses nets to capture fish. These are known as gill netters and rarely exceed 135 feet in length. The nets form a wall that entangles the prey by entangling their gill on the webbing. This method has declined in recent years. The best known gill net fisheries are those of the European herring and the Japanese Pacific salmon industries.

A fourth group of vessels uses hooks and lines instead of nets. The most efficient of these methods is the Japanese long-line process. Many small and varied boots are used around the world to set traps, nets, or lines.

*A purse seiner* (opposite, left), using a power block, draws the net together. *Otter boards* hang to the side of a trawlnet (opposite, right) as the gear is pulled on board the American vessel, Voyager.

*The mesh size limits the fish taken in* **gill nets.** *An opaleye* (above) *and a shark* (left) *have been caught in nets that a smaller fish could escape.*

95

# Chapter VIII. Farming the Sea

When our distant ancestors first recognized that hunting took too much time, depended on chance, and depleted the wildlife of an area, agriculture was invented. In the past 10,000 years we have learned to irrigate, fertilize, and develop hardy breeds of grain and stock. An acre of land, scientifically farmed, is far more useful in human terms than an agriculturally idle one. Man's energy is added to that of the sun to produce more and better food. Yet thousands of years after we abandoned hunting on land as an efficient method of obtaining food, we continue to pursue the creatures of the sea with the attitudes of cavemen.

At first we were prevented from extending our agricultural efforts into the sea. Because of hundreds of generations of careful observation and experience, we could determine what conditions were ideal for terrestrial animals and plants. Our understanding of the sea was, and still is, inadequate to permit the farming of all but a few organisms. Intensified research has come at a critical time.

> **"The better we learn to hunt, the faster we are able to eliminate more species of fish."**

Farmed land, domesticated animals, and creatures plucked from the sea are not meeting the world's need for food. Now we must change our philosophy, progressively stop hunting in the sea, and expand the ocean's living resources.

The new attitude has nothing in common with developing better fishing techniques. When we stalk our prey with satellites and lure fish to the kill with electricity, we are still hunting. The better we hunt, the faster some animals cease to exist. Ocean farming — mariculture — can protect the natural stock in the sea as well as vastly supplement our food supply.

The ocean farmer harvests only what he has grown. Nothing is lost from the sea. Man does not have to search miles for his food—animals raised in coastal pens are accessible. Domesticated animals produce more offspring. Domesticated animals are fed the best foods and grow quicker.

Even though a few marine animals have been cultured for centuries, we know relatively little about mass production of the living resources of the sea. Mariculture is an exciting adventure. For the first time in thousands of years we have the opportunity to develop a new food supply. The challenges are enticing: we know almost nothing about the diseases that could rob a farmer of his fish. Can we devise parasite and bacterial controls that will not interrupt the life cycles of other animals? What conditions can be produced to make life in a pen tolerable for an ocean animal? If we imitate nature and use the coastal areas for breeding grounds, what alternate areas can be set aside for the continuation of the natural populations? We can't eliminate all the wild species so we can totally farm the sea.

Even if we meet the challenges of mariculture beyond present expectations, the ocean, like the land, can only feed a yet unknown but limited number of people, even at its maximum productivity. As we create techniques for farming the sea, we must simultaneously work to limit world population and to reduce food needs.

*Turtle farms* on Grand Cayman Island are attempting to perfect methods of mariculture so that young turtles (opposite) can be bred in captivity.

## Grow Your Own

Legend says that the 300-year-old Japanese practice of oyster farming was started by a lord who moved from Wakayama to Hiroshima. He carried oysters from his former home to set in a bay near his new lands. His neighbors there had placed bamboo fences in the water to protect their clam beds from roving bat rays. Soon the fences were speckled with tiny oysters, called spat because it was thought that young oysters were blown out of the mouths of adults.

Fishermen in the bay tried to move the attached spat to other waters. When the larvae didn't survive, it was concluded that certain conditions had to exist for successful oyster growth. The water temperature can range only between 59° and 86° F. The tides must freqently change the water but must not be so swift as to tear the animals from their moorings. A supply of phytoplankton

In Japanese mariculture, **scallop cages** (above) must be changed after two years in water.

The **vertical culture** of oysters allows more shellfish to be raised than the old way, which limited the culture to the bottom. Strings of spat plates are suspended from rafts (below left).

**Glass floats** (below) mark vertical strings of oyster spat. The strings will be pulled up after two years and the plates replaced by new ones.

has to be available as food. To this day, oyster farmers rely on these determinations to guide the management of their crops.

Until 1923 the farmers placed roof tiles and abandoned shells on the bottom to collect spat. At that time it was determined that the free-swimming larvae would attach to strings of shells that dangled from the surface. This method provides better water circulation for the growing oysters and space for more spat to be cultivated. More of the young survive on the free-hanging strings because they are high above their worst enemy— the bottom-crawling starfish.

Most Japanese growers do not collect their own spat but buy "seed" already deposited on plates. In the past over half the Japanese seed was sent to the United States for culture. This is no longer necessary. Oyster farmers in Puget Sound have studied the Japanese techniques and now collect their own spat. Each summer, oyster larvae are collected in the Puget Sound waters to begin a life cycle that will last for one to three years. At that time the strings are pulled up, and the oysters harvested and sent to market. Oysters are ideal domesticated animals. They are easy to collect, grow rapidly, and require small living areas. Their culture may soon be even easier with the recognition that sewage can be diverted into special ponds to support algal growth. Oysters, seeded into the pond, graze on the algae. Marine biologists theorize that a 50-acre pond could provide the final stage of sewage treatment for a city of 11,000 and an annual crop of 1 million pounds of shellfish.

Development of private oyster cultivation reduces the impact of overharvesting on natural beds. Many of the spat would not survive in the wild for lack of a surface upon which to settle. Oysters cannot be cultivated where the bottom is too muddy, where silt would suffocate natural populations.

**Shrimp culture** has been successfully combined with warm-water effluent from the Turkey Point Power Plant (above) in Florida.

**Postlarval shrimp** are cultured in large ponds (below) and rapidly increase in size because warm water enhances their growth rate.

# Highly Cultured Shrimp

Shrimp are the basis for tempura, Japan's national dish. Natural supplies never meet the demand. It made economic sense to mariculturists to tackle shrimp farming as one of their first tasks. Thirty years of experimentation has brought such success to farmers of kuruma shrimp that they can afford to release surplus shrimp to natural grounds as a boon to local fishermen.

Egg-carrying females are captured and placed in saltwater tanks that imitate the natural shallow bays where the animals breed. Within 24 hours the water in the tanks usually becomes pink and foam appears on the surface an an indication that the two or three females in the tank have each produced their expected 300,000 to 1,000,000 eggs. For 12 days the larvae, called nauplii, are not fed. Thereafter they receive a different diet for each stage of their life. Initially fertilizers are added to the rearing tanks to stimulate the growth of algae—shrimp baby food. Later brine shrimp and then clams and fish supplement their diet. At the postlarval stage, the young take up a bottom existence, burrowing in the sand at the bottom of their tanks. The water circulation is kept swift to prevent cannibalism and to keep oxygen levels high. Disease and parasites do not present serious problems to the shrimp farmer. Between 60 and 100 percent of the infant shrimp survive their stay down on the farm and find their way to a kitchen.

Shrimp are the only cultivated marine food that is considered tastier than the wild variety. Home-grown kuruma may sell for as much as $10 a pound in Tokyo. Shrimp destined for odori, an extraordinary dish, bring at least $1.50 each. Odori shrimp are expensive because they must be absolutely fresh. The dish is considered a failure if the mouth parts of the animal are not moving about as the diner picks at it with his chopsticks.

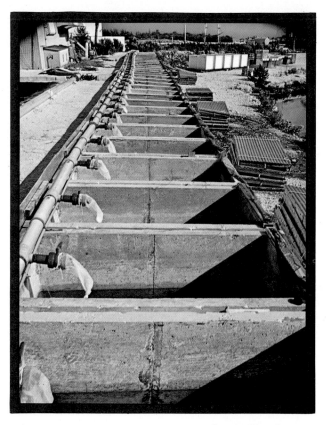

After hatching in the laboratory, **juvenile shrimp** (below) are stocked in the **culture tanks** (above), protected from predators.

Americans import half the shrimp they eat. Profiting from Japanese experience, several companies in the U.S. and Europe have started their own farms, especially in French Brittany and in Florida where legislation provides for leasing of public waters for private maricultural use. Costs are currently higher than the Japanese and since Americans will not pay as much for the tasty seafood, shrimp farming in the U.S. is not as attractive a business as it is elsewhere. However, predictions suggest that cultivated shrimp soon will be cheaper than chicken.

## Hot Fish

Anyone who has tried to keep a saltwater aquarium thriving has had a glimpse into the difficulties facing farmers of marine fin fish. Freshwater fish have been raised in hatcheries for at least 2000 years, but this is not the case for saltwater fish; the intricacies of maintaining proper salt balances and temperature and avoiding infections at the egg and larval stages have made management of mariculture ponds a tricky proposition.

The Japanese, whose island life-style traditionally sent them to the sea for food, have achieved success in raising a true ocean fish —the yellowtail. One-third of the yellowtails marketed in Japan are cultured fish. The farms' annual yield is as much as 126 tons of fish per acre. An advanced pig farm produces only 25 tons of live pigs per acre in the same amount of time.

One fish that is a commercial success, to the tune of a million-dollar-a-year catch in Florida alone, seems to be one of the best bets for the cultivation of an ocean fish. Pompano have great potential because they grow rapidly, don't have a highly specialized diet, and can tolerate the abrupt environmental changes that often occur in artificial ponds. So far the pompano business is an experimental one. Lack of knowledge about their reproductive life has made it impossible to get them to breed in captivity. Young fish are caught in beach nets to stock the ponds. The fry are fed commercial trout food by mechanized dispensers. So far, pompano have been raised in coastal pens. Shortage of coastal space is a problem in Florida. It has been suggested that the use of floating cages to hold the fish out at sea would expand the surface area available for fin-fish farms.

British researchers have coupled sole and plaice farms with warm water discharges from coastal power plants. The heated water allows sole to be raised farther north than they usually range and speeds their growth to the degree that they are ready for market a full year sooner than if they were raised in their natural cool water habitat.

Building power plants where the sea can be used as a coolant is widespread. It's important to consider that the use of ocean water for this purpose may be far more detrimental to the ocean ecosystem than could ever be offset by its secondhand use in fish culture.

The various mariculture projects will never be able to convert all the potentially lethal or thermal pollution to beneficial use for man.

*Young pompano* come to maturity in coastal rearing tanks (opposite above), where water is piped in (opposite bottom) from the ocean.

*The expensive* **pompano** *(below) live in coastal waters from Massachusetts to Brazil.*

## Tasty Cannibal

Lobsters are ill-tempered, solitary beasts. A tank containing several will soon hold only one—the biggest. The major frustration facing lobster farmers is that their charges persist in eating each other before they can be sent to market. One solution to the cannibal problem may be in a pheromone—a hormone released outside the body that acts on another individual.

During mating, male lobsters are noticeably docile due to the presence of an antiaggression pheromone secreted by the female. Isolation of this chemical would help the lobster business by eliminating the need for expensive, individual cages for maturing lobsters. Biologists at the Massachusetts State Hatchery have succeeded in raising lobster to 10 years of age. They have shown that nature takes about six years to grow a marketable

*Blue lobsters* represent a genetic mistake that breeders are utilizing. It is impossible to tag lobsters as they lose the tag with each molt; the blue beasts are easy to spot by researchers.

specimen, while rearing under ideal conditions reduces this time to under two years.

Lobsters carry their skeletons on the outside. In order to grow, they must shed their rigid outer shell in a process known as molting. During the first three weeks of life when the lobster young double in size almost weekly, they molt once a week before they settle to the bottom to seek dark hiding places.

The time when the larvae are free-floating is the most dangerous for them. Tides may carry them out to deep water and death. Ninety percent will become food for larger animals. Only one-tenth of one percent will survive. In this stage of lobster life mariculture improves on nature.

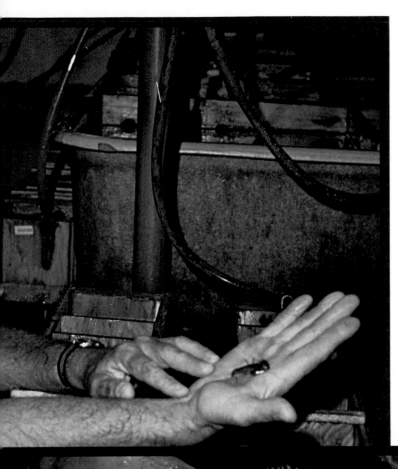

Cultivation begins with the capturing of egg-bearing females. Once the eggs are hatched, the young are collected on screens that filter water from the mother's tank. The larvae are placed in fiberglass rearing tanks where a steady diet of minced clams inhibits cannibalism. Over 30 percent will survive to the fourth molt. Usually the fourth-molt youngsters are released into the wild to supplement natural populations.

Lobster growers are not true farmers because they do not have control over their herds. They are more like ranchers since they release their stock to fend for themselves. Use of antiaggression hormones and innovation in cage design should bring the lobster off the open range to domestication.

*Tiny lobsters* (left) *are at the mercy of their environment. Mariculture increases their chance of survival by a large percentage. A* **female lobster** (*below*) *carries her eggs for a year.*

## Turtle Soup

Sailors long at sea used to suffer many dietary diseases. The length of their voyages was limited by how long their bodies could withstand lack of vitamins and fresh meat. Some historians believe that colonization of the Caribbean could not have taken place if it weren't for the green turtle. When sailors starved, the hard-shelled reptile meant life. Hundreds of turtles were killed as they came ashore to lay eggs or were taken alive to be carried away in the holds of ships.

Exploitation of the turtle continues today. Their meat and eggs are a favorite meal for many people of the southwest Pacific or the Indian Ocean. Turtle soup is traditionally

*Turtles on Grand Cayman Ranch (above) are protected from man and beast until they reach maturity when they are released **to feed** (below) on natural pastures of the continental shelf.*

the opening course at British royal banquets and at the meals offered by the Lord Mayor of London. The raw material comes from the Seychelles Islands. Collectors seeking tortoise shell for jewelry have also contributed to putting all seven known species of sea turtles on the endangered list.

Dr. Robert Schroeder, director of the world's first turtle ranch, is attempting to save the green turtle from extinction and to salvage a source of food for man by raising turtles on one of their last remaining rookeries on Grand Cayman Island, British West Indies. Eggs are taken from native breeding grounds in Costa Rica and Ascension Island and flown to the Grand Cayman ranch. Since the natural populations are diminishing so quickly and natural supplies of eggs are small, Dr. Schroeder is expending most of his efforts in encouraging his own turtles to breed.

The Grand Cayman experiment was not started exclusively for turtle conservation. The ultimate aim is to make a profit by obtaining food from the animals so the wild populations will be left alone.

## Sea Steak

Abalone steak has been called the filet mignon of the sea, not only because it is delicious but also because, in most parts of the world, its wholesale price is higher than that of prime cuts of beef.

The abalone fishery in the United States was begun in the early 1850s by Chinese nationals. Because they were not divers, most of their catch came from the intertidal zones or from shallow waters. Since the deepwater abalone communities were not harvested, they provided ample catches for helmeted divers from the 1930s. In 1966 a situation developed in the California abalone industry that was soon to be repeated in many other abalone fisheries. The catch in that year amounted to 2.5 million pounds—the largest ever. Since then the take has dwindled due to overharvesting.

A man who once wrote a college paper demonstrating the impossibility of farming abalone is now eating his words along with a steady diet of the shellfish. He and two other researchers oversee a 25'x45' structure that shelters a million abalone and insulates them from fluctuations in their diet of algae.

Abalone farming illustrates that mariculture has advantages beyond replenishing the sea. It is safer and can be less expensive than hunting. Abalone "hunters" must invest in boats and endure the hazards of guiding their vessels near the craggy rocks that abalone prefer. Hardy divers scour the bottom in frigid water for these delectable snails. Many of the abalone that remain are no longer found in easily accessible areas. Weather conditions limit abalone hunting to only a third of the days a year. Meanwhile, the abalone farmers leisurely watch over their tanks for three years and then proceed to harvest a drained tank without risking the dangers faced by their old-fashioned competitors.

*Experimental stations* (above) perfect the breeding of abalone. Mariculture operations include use of *cement structures* (below) in the sea to provide substrate for wild populations.

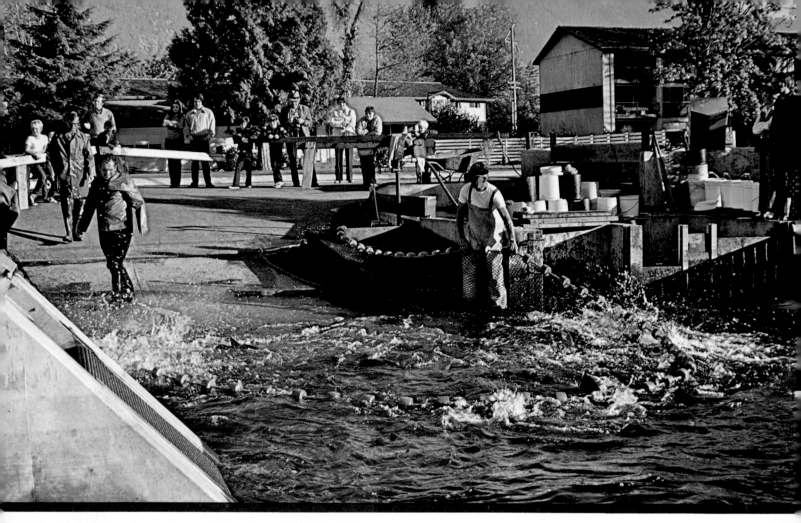

*Salmon* that are the fastest growing and healthiest are selected and pulled from the tank (above).

*Eggs* are milked from the best females (below) and mixed with sperm to produce "super salmon."

## Super Salmon

Many chicken generations ago, a hen laid only about a dozen eggs before she stopped to hatch her chicks. With the help of genetics, chickens are now bred that continuously lay eggs—up to 200 a year. The mechanism that created a new breed of chickens depends upon allowing mating to take place only between birds that have particular, desirable traits. After many generations, quality will breed true—all subsequent offspring will display the valued characteristics.

Scientists at the University of Washington are bringing man's knowledge of barnyard genetics to the fish farm by using the unique breeding behavior of the salmon. Since these migratory fish mate only at the site where they were hatched, creating a new hatching sea would ensure that only certain fish mated.

In 1947 university scientists released fingerling salmon into an artificial pond that led into a network of streams to the Pacific.

The earliest returning, fastest growing, and healthiest females were isolated from the remainder. They were bred with the most desirable males. No other salmon were allowed to reproduce. After 18 years of selective breeding, the salmon have increased in average weight from 10.8 to 12 pounds and are an inch longer than their ancestors. Over half the salmon now mature within three years. Egg production is up 10 percent.

Although the university salmon are special fish, they are not pampered. Their pond is as polluted as any other and no tears are shed if some of them don't survive long enough to spawn. One of the aims of the project is to produce hardy fish able to withstand environmental problems. Already the university fish have a 30 percent better chance of surviving their three or four years at sea than fish that have not had the advantages of a college background.

The amount of time it took to achieve the super salmon is a handicap to the project. If mariculture efforts were given time and support equivalent to agricultural research, more practical sea-farming operations could be expected. But mariculture is new and investments in research small. Since most fish take two to three years to mature, a 20-generation experiment would take 60 years to complete. A technique called gynogenesis has been developed by Colin Purdom in Britain. He has used sperm cells to stimulate egg development which do not impart their genes to the young. The females' desirable characteristics will show up in all the young, thus shortening the time required to develop a breeding population.

*Tagged salmon* will be easy to spot when they return from their stay at sea.

# Housing Project

The largest part of the ocean's bottom is covered by mud, and except for the burrowing animals, all the sea's creatures suffer from a severe housing shortage. Stationary organisms need a solid surface for attachment—the more surface, the more growth. Fish lack areas in which they can hide from their predators and are more easily gobbled up in the open than when they can escape into a sheltered area. Divers have often noticed that fish congregate around wrecked ships and the underwater structures associated with the petroleum industry, which are artificial oases where they find shelter and food. They may feel secure there simply because of a fish behavioral trait that scientists call thigmotrophism—a desire to associate with solid objects.

Old streetcars and horse racing have a great deal to do with good fishing in one area off the southern California coast. Fish and game administrators there have used state revenues from racing to finance the building of reefs from the bodies of abandoned automobiles and streetcars. The artificial reefs provide a substrate for algae to grow and give fish protection from predators.

The project was started in response to a decline in the so-called sport fishing catches that could be related to a similar decline in natural refuges for fish. Kelp beds along the southern California coast used to supply ample shelter and food for many varieties of fish. The kelp beds themselves have dwindled in recent years. The scientists hoped that the kelp could be reestablished on the artificial reefs. If the kelp would grow, hiding places would be increased, and food supplies for all the members of the food chain improved. They wanted to give the fish both room *and* board.

The first reef was composed of 20 old automobile bodies. They were placed in 50 feet of water off the Los Angeles coast at Malibu. After only a few months, the average population of the reef was about 10,000 semiresident fish. Powerful fish such as kelp bass, sand bass, and sheepshead were always present. A bed of kelp appeared naturally on the artificial reef within a few month's time.

Once it was shown that the population of fish was increasing, the scientists tried to determine the favorite housing material of the fish. Would they prefer homes made from old cars or from some other inexpensive material? Experimental reefs were composed of old streetcars, additional ones were made of old cars, and still others from concrete structures of various shapes. One final reef was added to the project at a later date: a reef made of quarry rock.

Population studies were done prior to the installation of the artificial reefs and then at intervals after they were constructed. Apparently the fish prefer stable, long-lived reefs and would much rather live in a stone house than in a deteriorating streetcar. Strangely enough, artificial reefs in the Mediterranean did not increase significantly the abundance of life in the area.

Well-organized artificial reefs could become a simple way to farm certain thinly populated areas. For the moment, they have been useful to science and to the so-called sport fishermen. Catches in the areas around artificial reefs are high, reflecting their increased productivity.

*An **artificial reef** is colonized. Fish (opposite left) have come to feed on small clumps of algae. Finally, colonization is complete (opposite right).*

*Artificial **streetcar reefs** (below) provide housing and food for small organisms and large fish in areas of the sea where shelter is sorely lacking.*

# Open-Sea Farming

It would seem that the open sea would be a cornucopia of seafood. After all it is in the open sea that we find the great schools of tuna and whales and other important seafood fish. Actually, when it comes to per acre food production, the great open spaces far from land are virtual deserts compared to coastal and reef areas.

Great abundance of life does not occur in the open sea, in part because of low nutrients, in part because of the lack of substrate. Organic nutrients fall to the bottom, far out of reach of the plants that must stay near the surface supply of sunlight. Unable to reach miles down into the sea, phytoplankton depend upon upwelling to bring natural fertilizer from the bottom where organic matter accumulates. Offshore drifts pull nutrient-rich waters to the surface only at some coastal areas. Conditions that create upwelling generally do not exist far out at sea. Since plant growth is low, fewer animals are supported than in nutrient-rich waters.

Mariculture experiments have not been carried out in the open sea, primarily because of its lack of natural productivity. Now, however, in the Virgin Islands where deep water is only a mile from shore, a system has been developed to create artificial upwelling. Pumps bring bottom water to surface tanks where the nutrients activate algae growth. Shellfish then feed on the plant life.

To put the St. Croix project to work in the open sea would not be prohibitively difficult. In fact, some ocean-mining techniques cause upwelling as a by-product of their activity. Scientists are watching open-sea mining projects to see whether or not there will be an increase in plant production.

The major problem of creating an open-sea oasis of plant and animal life is containment.

No farmer wants to watch his market-ready crops swim away or be taken on another's lines. Some suggest that bottom water could be pumped into a coral atoll. Nutrients in the water would make the basis for a lush community into which food fish could be introduced. The abundance of food in the lagoon and the natural barrier presented by the atoll would discourage wandering.

Another method of fencing in fish is by "bubble" fences. A mechanism is placed on the bottom to encircle the open-sea farm. It releases air, creating a wall of bubbles. This may be able to contain some species of fish, although sharks have been known to cross such bubble barriers.

Mariculture at great depths does not seem likely—plant production is nonexistent there because of a lack of light. But futuristic scientists propose that solar energy

*Salmon are raised in a deep bay near Seattle (above). Floats mark the top of a huge net that encircles the salmon farm. The entire operation could easily be adapted for the open sea.*

*Creation of **fish "huts"** (opposite) would increase the survival rate in the open sea by providing housing, food, and a substrate for sessile organisms.*

cells that would carry the sun to the bottom of the sea could be tested. Photosynthesis would then take place, and presumably animals would migrate downward to feed on the plants. A first step was made in that direction in 1965. Productivity measurements were made by our oceanaut-scientists of Conshelf III in two cubes of water installed in 335 feet of depth, one in the dark and the other one artificially illuminated. It may seem farfetched to think of divers tending fields of bottom-growing plants but in the world of the ocean we seem to be able to ask "Why not?" more easily than "Why?"

# Chapter IX. Marine Medicine Chest

Poison darts and stinging cells are only two weapons evolution has given marine animals. Some, like the nematocysts in coelenterates, are specialized cells used to stun victims, making food capture an easier chore for animals that can't swiftly pursue prey. The venomous spines of some fish fulfill a protective need. Man and fish alike soon learn to avoid creatures that can cause pain or death.

One group of people seeks these irritating animals, delighting in locating specimens that most take great steps to avoid. They are marine pharmacologists, who recognize that in each dangerous chemical produced in the sea is a potentially beneficial drug. For example, a component in a certain jellyfish's sting accelerates heartbeat. A purified dilu-

---

**"In each dangerous toxin produced in the sea is a potentially beneficial drug."**

---

tion of the substance stimulates the heart of a patient suffering from cardiac arrest. The trick is to tame the poison.

Of the drugs presently available only one percent comes from the sea, partially because researchers have been kept busy enough examining chemicals from land sources. Another reason marine chemicals have been ignored as pharmaceuticals is the difficulty in maintaining a standardized population from which to extract the drugs. (When water chemistry changes so do the bodily fluids of marine organisms.) Mariculture may enable drug firms to establish stocks from which to draw dependable supplies of biologically active chemicals. New families of antibiotics have already been isolated and studied. Modern drug laboratories

use computers to enumerate all the possible chemicals related to a given family that could be synthesized, but they need input that only nature can supply.

Hundreds of marine species are poisonous. Researchers face a formidable task even deciding where to begin a survey of possible drugs in the sea. Ancient medical records sometimes provide startlingly accurate clues. A biblical dietary law states, "These ye shall eat of all that are in the waters; all that have fins and scales ye shall eat, and what ever hath not fins and scales ye may not eat; it is unclean." This advice has a basis in fact. Many fish with poisonous flesh belong to the group Plectognathi, which lacks scales.

Whenever a disease is absent or restricted in a certain locality, an examination of diet and customs of the people may reveal sound medical advice. Cancer is not commonly found among some Polynesian Islanders. According to medical custom on many of the islands, cancer victims are fed the internal fluids of a sea worm. Researchers at the University of Hawaii collected information about the cure, extracted substances from several varieties of marine worms, and fed the materials to mice with induced cancer. Malignant cell growth was inhibited in 60 percent of the mice.

An extract from the ordinary clam has a similar effect on cancerous growth. However, no antitumor activity is shown by the substance if the clam was raised in polluted waters. It would be a regrettable loss if we contaminated the drugs in our marine medicine chest just when we finally pried it open.

*The **needle-sharp spines** of the lionfish are hidden in delicate, lacelike fins. A dangerous toxin is ejected through the spines.*

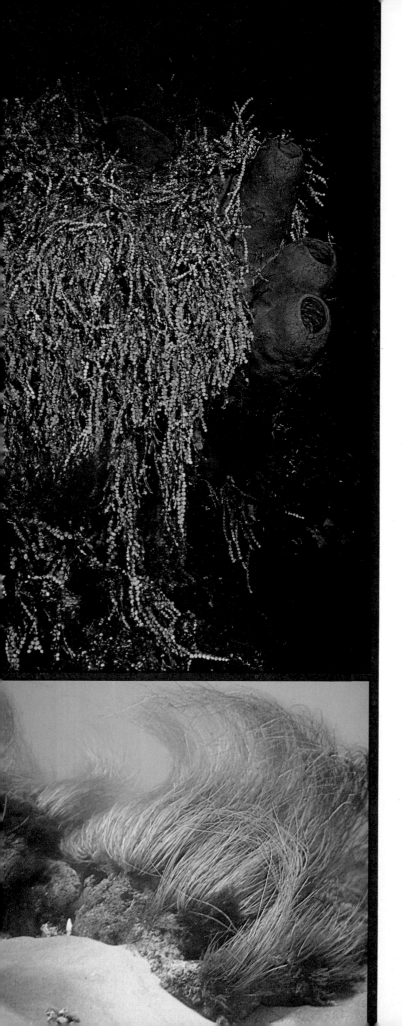

## Herbal Cures

The earliest record of the effect of algae toxins was written by Moses. He described it by saying the waters turned to blood and stank from dying fish. We now know that dinoflagellates cause red tides, killing fish by depriving them of oxygen, and by a toxin they produce. These poisons, when diluted, stop the growth of most types of bacteria and may give relief to sufferers of bacterial diseases in the future. The contents of penguins' stomachs support this hunch.

Scientists on an antarctic expedition found that the intestines of penguins were remarkably free of bacteria that usually inhabit animal digestive organs. Clearly, an antibiotic substance was present. Its source was traced through the birds' food from their main diet of small crustaceans, called krill, to the krill's food of green algae. From the plant was isolated halosphaerin, a strong antibiotic.

The ancient Japanese cure for intestinal worms is ingestion of red seaweed, also an alga. The modern cure for the same affliction is a dose of kainic acid. Analysis of the seaweed, stimulated by its apparent healing abilities, enabled pharmacologists to isolate kainic acid and to prepare a commercial medicine for use by worm-infested individuals living far from the ocean and natural sources of seaweed.

Alginic acid from kelp has a unique characteristic. It rids the body of radioactive strontium. Since this isotope of strontium is the most dangerous to human life of all the components in fallout from atomic explosions, this could be an important lifesaving discovery. A different alginic compound holds the heavier particles in liquid medicines in suspension so that those who forget to "shake first" still get a proper portion of medicine rather than a spoonful containing only the dissolving medium.

It seems curious to seek additional healing
agents when doctors already have an array
of pills from which to pick their prescrip-
tions. We already have antibiotics available
for use against many of the organisms that
marine plants can destroy so why should
expensive research be undertaken to add to
them? The best answer is found in a fungus
that proliferates in a sewage outfall off Sardinia. It is the source of cephalothin—an
antibiotic with properties similar to penicillin. Its most valuable asset is that it is effective against bacteria that have developed
penicillin immunity.

*Green algae* (opposite top) is common in the Caribbean. *Fucus* (right), also known as rockweed, is
a prominent brown algae in both hemispheres.

*Eel grass* (opposite bottom) is one of the few true
vascular plants in the sea.

*Red algae* (below) is useful as a medicinal in Japan, primarily as a cure for worms.

# The Healing Sting

At least 70 species of coelenterates—sea anemones, coral, and jellyfish—have some toxic effect on man. Some like the sea nettle, a jellyfish common in coastal Atlantic waters, cause no more than an irritating sting. Others (the sea wasp jellyfish is the best example) can cause death. Numerous chemicals with medicinal properties have been isolated from members of this large marine family. The toxins that cause paralysis and death have the greatest potential in combating cardiac and muscular diseases and perhaps in fighting epilepsy.

Presently, however, the isolation of coelenterate toxins has greatest importance to divers. Development of immunization against the most deadly of the stings would be a great protective measure. Antitoxins, if available, would relieve one of the greatest dangers to underwater enthusiasts.

Most sea anemones are less toxic than the species of coral and jellyfish that can harm man. The exception is a South Vietnam variety called con nhum by locals and hell's fire anemone in English—for good reason. A burning sting is felt immediately when a swimmer touches the nematocysts of the anemone. Within a few hours, depending on the sensitivity of the individual, swelling, redness, and ulcerations develop around the area of the sting. Treatment for the sting has not been developed beyond the native use of lime powder and coconut oil. It is believed that the venom will have potential as a pharmaceutical after extensive research.

*Two species of anemones* (opposite) *whose nematocysts can't penetrate human skin still contain toxins dangerous to soft-bodied marine animals.*

*Jellyfish* (right and above) *often harbor biologically active chemicals that hold great promise as drugs for the treatment of muscular diseases.*

# Venomous Cone Snails

Cone snail shells are best sellers in souvenir shops, partially because of the beautiful pattern, glaze, and color that characterize many varieties. They are a bit more expensive than other shells because some are difficult to locate. Hard-sell clerks emphasize that the shell is so dangerous to collect that divers avoid it. This makes for a good story but is usually not the case since the shells are often collected only after the animal with its poison darts has abandoned its home.

When a suitable prey falls within the range of the cone snail, it ejects its venomous darts to penetrate the skin of the victim. We could almost speak of the cone snail as biting its prey since the dart is a highly evolved modification of a tooth. The toxin contained in *Conus geographus* is a muscle relaxant so strong that animals injected with it relax, stop breathing, and die. The toxins may be helpful to individuals whose muscles are in a state of convulsion. But it's never wise to jump to generalizations when dealing with living systems.

Just as researchers were about to classify cone snail venom as a relaxant, they discovered that the species known as *C. magus* immobilizes its victims with a chemical that causes muscles to contract violently. The venom of one snail could perhaps be an antidote for the other. Medicine has an additional need for muscle stimulators. The patient can die when nerves that excite muscles and stimulate them to move are damaged, and automatic systems like breathing or heartbeat are impaired. A drug from *C. magus* might restore contractibility to muscles that have been damaged by injury.

Like the cone snail, clams, oysters, squid, octopuses, and abalone are molluscs. Extracts from particular members of these groups are effective as antiviral drugs. Called paolin, Chinese for abalone extract, components of these materials have been shown to protect laboratory mice infected with influenza and polio virus.

*The spines* of the sea urchin Diadema setosum (above) pose a threat to divers, causing a reaction when their toxin is injected under the skin.

The venom of the **cone snail** (opposite) is of vast interest to researchers seeking new medicines. The toxin from one is an effective muscle relaxant.

*Pedicellaria* on the sea urchin (below) contains a toxin that is injected by means of a fanglike projection in the clasping organ.

# Drugs in Search of a Disease

Only a small percentage of the plants and animals in the ocean have been examined for potential drugs. After a tedious process involving extraction and purification of such chemicals, an even longer path lies ahead. What will the chemical do for a sick human being? Scientists send the new chemical running through the bloodstream of laboratory animals, some sick and some well, and wait for the results. A measure of what we might find if we knew more about yet-to-be-examined marine organisms is found in the many properties of just one class of extracts from one organism—the sea cucumber.

When attacked, some sea cucumbers discharge their internal organs and entangle the offender (eviscerate). Mucus that covers the organs is toxic and contains a compound known as holothurin. The substance has a bewildering range of activities. It retards growth of fruit flies, causes abnormal development in sea urchins, prevents regeneration in flatworms, and halts the growth of several types of tumors in mice. In all cases, holothurin has inhibited cell growth. One of the most bewildering medical problems today is how to stop cell division gone crazy—cancer. Maybe the sea cucumber will provide an answer to the cancer mystery.

Experiments on mice show that holothurin stimulates the heart in a manner similar to digitalis, a cardiac drug synthesized from the foxglove plant. Sea cucumber chemicals are also being considered as anesthetics.

We speak of wonder and miracle drugs as if our utilization of organic chemicals began yesterday. Holothurin has been known to natives of Guam for generations. They squeeze sea cucumbers into crevices and pools where fish are known to hide. Soon the drugged fish float to the surface and are easily caught as they flounder about.

*Holothurin, a useful drug, is isolated from the mucous covering of the organs of the sea cucumber (opposite), released during evisceration (below).*

# Fishy Treatments

Suicide in Japan is an honorable way out of a dishonorable situation. An ocean fish that is a prized delicacy is also an often-used means to a quick release from life. The skin, gonads, or viscera, depending upon the season of the year, of the pufferfish are so toxic to human beings that death can occur within 15 minutes after they've been eaten. There is no antidote.

Over 100 cases of lethal pufferfish poisoning are reported every year in Japan. Some of these are suicides; some are accidentally caused when the fish are eaten by ignorant victims. Most pufferfish poisonings until recently were a result of eating sushi fugu, raw pufferfish, a delicacy found in some Japanese restaurants. The incidence of death from puffer poison was so common that the government now licenses only college-trained cooks to prepare the puffer specialities.

A mixture of puffer gonads and sake, a Japanese liquor, is said to increase virility. Drinking the concoction is like playing Russian roulette. There is no way of assessing the degree of toxin present or the chance of dying, without sampling it first.

The essense of puffer poison is tetrodotoxin —a powerful blocking agent that acts on muscles and the nerves that govern movement and receive pain. Tetrodoxin is commercially available for use as an antispasm treatment for epileptics and to relieve the agony of terminal cancer.

In contrast to the puffer, the flesh of some venomous fish can be eaten without fear. Their danger and possible medicinal use to man is concentrated not in the tissues but in special glands or spines. The fisherman's cry of "Nohu! Nohu!" signals the presence of such a fish in the offshore reefs of Polynesia and means that an unlucky wader has stepped on a stonefish. In an extreme case,

*The **lionfish** (opposite) flares its venomous fins. The fearless behavior of a **scorpionfish** (left) indicates the poisonous spines serve as a deterrent to most predators. The **porcupinefish** (above) is a relative of the pufferfish.*

an hour after the onset of the first symptoms, the excruciating pain will cease as the heart stops and death brings relief.

Some say they are experts at locating the stonefish. But such expertise must be based on intuition. The fish hides under the sand, only poking out its terrible spines when disturbed. Then, a needlelike projection pushes out of a covering sheath to inject a milky venom into the hapless victim.

A chemical with such profound effects on cells is bound to have a medicinal use. It causes an abrupt increase in blood pressure, so seems a likely aid in the treatment of blood-pressure disorders.

# The Heart of a Hag

The animals that are the most curious to us are those that are seemingly different in all respects from ourselves. But because all forms of life must carry on most of the same functions, careful study of lower forms of life can often provide clues to what can go wrong with our own physiology.

The sex of a human embryo is determined at fertilization by the presence of one or another of a certain chromosome in the sperm. In one kind of marine worm, the peanut worm, the sex of the offspring is decided well after birth. The male lives inside the female and fertilizes eggs that will develop into free-swimming larvae. If the newly hatched worms happen to land for a moment on their mother's nose, they will develop into males. Only those that swim directly away will become females. A growth and sex-regulating hormone secreted by the proboscis of the mother inhibits development in larvae that encounter it. When the chemical is extracted from the female and placed on cancer cells in the laboratory, cell growth stops. The chemical, called bonellinin, may become an important cancer or birth control drug.

Our heartbeat is regulated by nervous impulses and an intriguing tissue within the heart itself called a pacemaker. If either the nerves to the heart or the pacemaker cease to function, heartbeat stops or becomes so erratic as to be useless. An electronic, transistorized pacemaker must be implanted. If the mechanism fails, so does the heart. A chemical from the hagfish may make electronic pacemakers obsolete.

Only one of the hagfish's three hearts is controlled by direct nerve connections to the brain. A chemical, eptatretin, stimulates and coordinates the beat of the other two. When mice with damaged cardiac nerves are given eptatretin, normal heartbeat is restored.

An octopus, on first glance, may not appear to be a deeply emotional or intelligent animal. They are, however, capable of learning and seem to express fear and anger. This has been confirmed by the experiences of divers who have lived some time with them. The brain of an octopus has some similarities to ours; yet it is simple enough to study with ease. Experiments on the brainy creature have helped drug addicts by furthering our understanding of what happens to a human mind burdened with drugs.

Of what is known about how a simple cell develops into a human adult, a great deal can be attributed to work with sea urchin eggs. Giant nerve cells as big as pencil leads that are found in the brains of squid have served the neurological researcher well. In fact almost any human organ or system in need of study will be found in a simpler, more convenient form in the sea.

*Extracts of the salivary glands of the **Australian spotted octopus** (left) contain one of the most powerful of known marine toxins.*

**A diver examines an octopus** (right). Healthy specimens of this animal are helpful to scientists probing the mysteries of the human brain.

# Chapter X. A Sea of Recreation

One of the greatest potentials the ocean has for mankind has little to do with oil or diamonds, pharmaceuticals, or even food. It is the opportunity to contemplate, enjoy, and explore this new realm.

Pleasure and peace of mind are not frivolous pursuits. We must not forget that the ultimate goal of civilization is not production or work for the sake of working and producing but rather the endeavor to fill the essential needs and to provide the ingredients of happiness: education, artistic emotions, freedom, health, leisure, and security. Today leisure time is expanding and retirement is coming sooner for many people. These additional time periods will allow us to replenish

---

**"The sea is the last unexplored frontier remaining on earth. It offers an unsurpassed adventure to those of us still willing to explore."**

---

our creative wellsprings and gain relief from the pressures of living in an overcrowded, industrialized society.

Cedric Wright in the Sierra Club book *Words from the Earth* suggests that sitting idly under a tree will begin "a vast healing" of an overworked mind. Today when campsites must be reserved weeks in advance and many recreation areas are as crowded as a downtown parking lot, Wright's statement might be more appropriately put: "Being near the sea, a vast healing begins."

On a sunny summer day, on a beach in New Jersey or southern California, there is little opportunity for idle pleasure. Tempers flare, dogs fight, and children get lost in a maze of beach umbrellas. The crowd overflows into nonbeach areas to trample on tide pools and sensitive biological areas.

In order to preserve the sea and its shore for less frantic leisure use, several changes have been made in government attitudes toward the use of coastal land. Both the U.S. and Japanese governments have set aside numerous areas as underwater parks and animal preserves. Those in Japan will be off limits to all fishing. Glass-bottom boats and small submarines will expose the beauty of the sea to nondiving tourists. Underwater hotels and restaurants are proposed. Some areas are being set aside as wilderness areas — off limits to all but the creatures that naturally inhabit the water. Dilapidated waterfront areas in many cities are being renovated to offer the public the beauty of an ocean view while they dine or shop. Floating and stationary platforms are proposed to increase coastal space for leisure activities.

Ocean recreation is much more than peaceful relaxation. The sea is the last unexplored frontier on earth. It offers an unsurpassed adventure to those still willing to explore. The very same crowds that are eagerly preparing to take advantage of such opportunities — and they already number in the hundreds of millions — must be thoroughly educated. Every single adult or teenager about to vacation on the seashore must learn a number of safety rules, read about the hazards and behavior of marine animals, and thoroughly understand that he must refrain from catching, touching, or even slightly disturbing any living thing on the beach, in the tide pools, or deeper in the ocean.

*The ocean offers a new world recreation. **Artist Andre Laban** (opposite) works with oil and canvas to capture underwater beauty.*

## Skimming the Surface

Water skiing was invented in the French Alps. That is not as improbable as it sounds. The Chasseurs Alpins, a select group of soldiers skilled in alpine warfare, including skiing, were the first to try skiing on water. After a bout of drinking, one group of "chasseurs" challenged another to try their skill behind a boat. The long, narrow snow skis failed to be practical, but the daredevils soon tried again with wider skis similar to those used today.

The first water ski was patented in 1924 by an American, Fred Waller. In his design, the tow rope was attached to the skis and the

skier had to hold on to another rope that was tied to the tips of the skis. Today 6 million water skiers glide over the surface of lakes and the ocean on fiberglass and laminated-wood skis that give them stability.

Water skiers soon tired of just being pulled behind a boat. They began to ski on one ski, go off high jumps, and speed through slalom courses with ease. Competitions are held yearly to determine the best skier in each of many events. With the development of fast, powerful speedboats, competitive skiers were given the ultimate challenge. Ski racers are commonly pulled at 60–90 miles an hour for up to 75 miles in grueling tests of endurance. Their speed only depends upon the roughness of the water. In perfect water conditions, the most daring try for the world's speed record—now more than 110 miles per hour. Jay Baverstock, an experienced competitor, described a fall he sustained while being pulled at over 90 miles an hour as hitting cement and rolling across it for what seemed like an eternity.

The agility of an experienced water skier, and the beauty with which he skims over the waves, was early seen as a form of entertainment for those who did not wish to try the sport themselves. In Florida one of the major attractions of the flourishing tourist business is the water-skiing ballet, performed in several beach communities in the state. Both competitions and ballets are demonstrations of unusual skill and draw large crowds.

Snow skiers need not depend upon a tow to pull them to the top of their favorite mountain. Ernest Hemingway said that anyone who wasn't man enough to climb a mountain didn't deserve to ski down it. Water skiers can't be so independent. Without a boat, they're sunk. A good portion of the 4.7 million recreational boats registered in the United States are used to pull water skiers.

A great number of the recreational motor boats are located in coastal states and are used on the ocean. They no doubt bring great pleasure and excitement to those millions who own them, but they have earned a bad reputation in other circles. Most pleasure boat associations caution their members to save nonbiodegradable trash for onshore disposal and to be considerate of others using the same waters. Nothing gives the pleasure motorboat men a worse name than the speeding, noisy boats that dart in and out in a busy marina, leaving a trail of beer cans and trash in their wake.

Quieter and cleaner than the powercraft are the sailing boats. They are too slow to pull water skiers, and they are unsuited to so-called sport and "game" fishing. Nevertheless, sailing is the sport of the "true" sailors; it offers to its fans the rare opportunity to forget the pressure of modern life and to struggle, with bare hands, against the natural forces of the winds and the sea.

One of the reasons that sailing appeals to some individuals is that it depends upon natural modes of propulsion. Sailing requires a keen understanding of nature: winds, waves, tides, and currents. Maneuvering even a small sailboat demands skills far beyond that needed to start the motor of a power boat or to man its helm.

Modern science and technology have helped develop new sailing thoroughbreds. These fascinating craft, such as hydrofoil catamarans, can reach speeds of 25 to 30 knots and, when close-hauled, move even faster than the wind, giving the speed-loving power fanatics a run for their money. Even so, the closest we can probably get to the soothing effects of the sea without going down into it is to spend a day sailing and challenging the forces of nature as they test the strengths of man and his sailing vessel.

## Fishing for Fun

To the commercial fisherman, the living resources of the sea represent his paycheck. To others, fishing offers a recreational outlet from the daily routine of life, a reason to be out of doors, to breathe clean, salt air, and to feel the spray of ocean breezes. One of the other reasons for the popularity of fishing is that the mute animals have a silent agony. To reassure one's conscience, it is said that they are cold-blooded and don't feel pain. Of course such beliefs are totally without foundation.

Recreational fishing is popular in virtually every nation that is close to water. A rod and reel, the angler's basic equipment, appear in a Chinese painting said to be from the period 1190–1230. Fishing is also an ancient and widely practiced form of recreation in Japan. Today, in the United States, well **over 9 million people fish for "fun."** In 1970, saltwater anglers caught over 700,000 tons of fish. This is significant compared to the 3 million tons landed by American commercial fishermen during the same year.

The qualities that fishermen admire in fish are primarily their ability to put up a good fight, and to a small degree their flavor when cooked. Along the Atlantic coast, the striped bass and the bluefish, or in the open sea, the Atlantic tarpon (weighing as much as 340 pounds), the swordfish, the black marlin, or the bluefin tuna (weighing up to 1800 pounds) are famed "fighters" and respected "game" fish. Some fishermen take only their quotas and have an enduring respect for the animals of the sea. Even so, we look forward to the day when a politician will realize that he will get more votes by his support of a fish sanctuary than by posing in a photograph with a giant dead fish that he and his buddies have caught just to prove that they are "good old boys."

# Surfers

Thanks to Hollywood movies popular in the late 1950s, the sport of surfing became synonomous with sun-bleached hair and beach parties. Youths far inland affected the "surfer" look and dreamed of moving to California. The most adventurous went on to Hawaii, the capital of surfing. The surfing enthusiasts were not part of a new wave as many of them thought, but practicing a sport of kings, 1000 years old.

Polynesians may have brought the first surf boards to Hawaii from beaches farther to the west, but it was on the islands of Oahu, Hawaii, and Maui that the sport took hold. The early boards were called olos and were made from a balsalike wood, wiliwili. The olos could only be used by royalty. The less desirable beaches and heavier, shorter boards (koas) were used by commoners. The long royal boards were up to 16 feet long and weighed over 100 pounds. Both men and women surfed.

In February 1778 a British ship under the command of Captain Cook sailed into view of the islands. One of the first things they spied was a tall Hawaiian, seemingly floating over the waves. Surfing continued as a popular pastime in the islands until 1821 when the first of the Calvinist missionaries arrived from Boston to put an end to what they considered the sinful, pagan activities of the Hawaiians. The mumu was designed to cover their bodies, and surfing was forbidden to all Hawaiians.

Not until the sport was recognized as an asset to tourism did it regain popularity. After World War II surfing really caught on, spreading from Hawaii to California and wherever else a ride could be coaxed from a wave. Soon a $12-million-a-year business centered in California was in full swing.

The wiliwili long boards are hardly recognizable next to today's surf boards. Polyurethane-filled, with fiberglass outer coverings, surf boards now incorporate the highest degree of hydrodynamic knowledge.

Some beaches are known all over the world as being consistently good for surfing. They are found mostly in Hawaii, California, and Australia. At each beach, the surf varies with

134

the weather and the time of year. Bottom formations reshape waves as they come into shore so there is a consistent directional break to all waves at a particular site.

The sport of surfing has become so popular that is has been brought to the desert. A man-made lagoon outside of Phoenix, Arizionia, covering 2.5 acres, is the setting for the artificial surf. Waves are produced through a hydraulic system housed in a 160-foot-long reservoir at the base of the lagoon. The water is pumped to a level in the reservoir and then released to develop into "spilling breaker" waves, which are up to five feet high and occur every 41 seconds.

*Enjoying the most exhilerating of aquatic sports,* **surfers** *"drop in" to the vertical wall of a wave.*

## Millions of Divers

Diving equipment has opened up the earth's last frontier for exploration by adventurers, photographers, businessmen, and housewives. The world of fish is now our world too. Since the introduction of the aqualung, the sport of underwater exploration has been taken up by a million enthusiasts in the United States alone. Diving is a challenging sport, unique in that it combines the use of skill and strength with self-control and aesthetic appreciation—exercise with educational opportunities. Hardly anyone diving in an area rich in marine life can resist the sudden need to learn about the new world that he sees before him.

Resorts that cater to the diver are springing up over the world. The favorite spots of eastern Americans are the coasts and islands of the Caribbean, where clear, warm water gives an undisturbed view of life on the reefs.

On St. John, in the Virgin Islands, an underwater sightseer has no problem finding interesting spots to visit. The National Park Service has extended its system of nature walks into the sea. An underwater trail has been designed so that experience with compressed-air diving equipment isn't necessary. The sightseer needs only a snorkle, flippers, and a mask. A 30-yard swim brings the first display into view—a brain coral. Near the coral is a plaque giving biological information about the exhibit. The trail continues around the bay, offering a glimpse into the marine world to all age groups. A typical day's visitors to the "walk" range in age from children to retired men and women.

Equipment for the diver continues to be improved. However, many of the recent innovations in breathing apparatus are not meant for the recreational diver. The newest apparatus features computerized, mixed-air systems that enable professional divers to go

to great depths for long periods of time. The physical limitations of the human body in the pressure of deep water are well known. Each foot of depth man gains in the sea will be won in physiological laboratories. There are no contests for amateur depth records—nor should there be.

The underwater leisure world is a young field. Innovations pop up every year as companies vie for the underwater dollar. The latest in such innovations is a line of recreational wet submersibles. In these, the normally equipped diver is carried about by the little battery-powered submarines, exposed to the water rather than being protected from it as he would be in a "dry" submersible.

*Such undersea habitats as **Hydrolab** (right) are available for rent to the vacationing diver.*

*Although mixed gas systems greatly extend the territory of professional divers, explorers (left) and recreational divers (below) rely on the safe and traditional **aqualung**.*

The sea provides many photographic subjects. **The eye of an octopus** (above) and the lens covering a **skate's eye** (below) are captured on film.

The artist's brush can rarely paint patterns as intriguing as those of **the coral** (opposite), which constructs a fragile combination of color and structure.

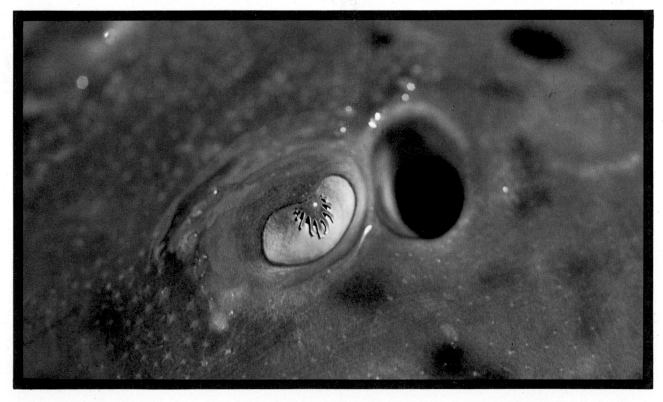

## Converting Spears to Cameras

Many divers take advantage of their time of freedom in the sea to hunt down and kill almost any ocean creature they find there. It is difficult to monitor the damage that hunting divers have inflicted on the marine populations, but in spearfishing contests, winners have perforated and brought back as much as a half a ton of fish in a single day. Over 850,000 spearfishing kits are sold each year in the world. There are known to be over 3 million spearguns presently owned. Undersea hunters are aiming their selective weapons precisely into the recesses that were the last refuges of coastal species against the fishermen's lines, nets, traps, and trawls. In 1936, when the first undersea explorers made their debut in the sea, crowds of fish came to welcome them; they soon understood that the intruder was there to spread destruction. After less than a year, fish were aware of man's real nature; the survivors migrated to less favorable areas where their lives and reproductive abilities are jeopardized. It takes only one year for one single spearfisherman operating every day to practically annihilate the bustling fish life of a one-mile stretch of coral reef.

The sport of stalking and killing animals is just as odious as the so-called big game fishing, since neither is motivated by the desire to catch choice food, and both end up by wasting large amounts of fish. Many spearfishermen have no knowledge of how to prepare what they have killed, others fear eating fish they think may be poisonous. The game, for them, is only killing in a fictional demonstration of virility.

We encourage spearfishermen to consider the new hunting technique that many land sportsmen have adopted. The prey is stalked; the hunt is on. But the animal is captured on film rather than killed. Underwater photography presents a challenge in itself. Furthermore, the hunter can share his pictures with nondiving friends and family.

## Seascapes

We have discovered in the volume *A Sea of Legends: Inspiration from the Sea* why the sea in the past had not fully inspired artists and poets. We also understand how rapidly this situation is changing.

The pioneer undersea painter was Zahr H. Pritchard, who accompanied William Beebe on his early expeditions and took his easel to the sea floor in 1919; one of

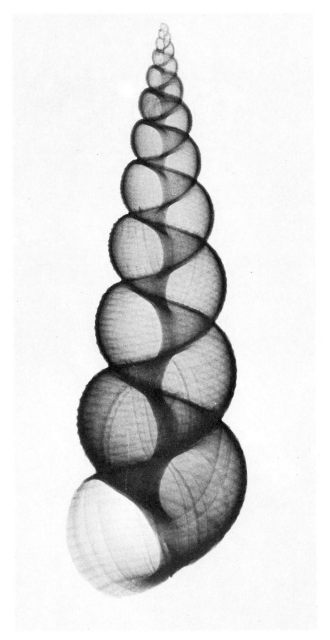

his spectacular modern followers is André Laban. Underwater artists found that salt water was more damaging to the canvas than to the paint. Some of them waterproof the canvas by boiling it in oil and turpentine. When they complete a painting, they return to the surface, wash the salt away, and varnish the work. One of them said that he did it all for the sake of truth, and for him truth is at the bottom of the sea.

Contemporary artists, who do not feel that it is necessary to get their canvas wet in order to receive inspiration from the ocean, have concentrated on the philosophical or emotional feelings the ocean elicits.

The work of two young women, although each is unique, serves to illustrate the interest that contemporary artists are taking in nature. One, Véjà Celmins, using pencil and graphite, depicts the surface of the sea. Hundreds of small waves seem to undulate over the paper. Nancy Graves, another young American artist, bases some of her large, pointillistic paintings on topographical and seismic studies of the sea floor. She has selected the ocean floor because of what she feels is her artistic obligation to respond to the historic moments of her generation. She feels that the exploration and elucidation of the sea is such a historic event.

After a decade or more of pop art culture, abstract artists are turning again to nature. The two artists just mentioned have selected the sea for inspiration in some of their work, but both also take inspiration from space: Celmins has given her interpretation of the surface of the moon and Graves has done paintings that use the Mariner photos of Mars as their basis. For both, outer space and the sea are equally exciting.

*Utility of design and simplicity of structure are revealed in **X rays of shells** (left and right).*

# Index

## ILLUSTRATIONS AND CHARTS:

Howard Koslow—16, 48-49.

## PHOTO CREDITS:

Gail Ash—27; Bos Kalis Westminster Group N.V.—31 (bottom); Bruce Coleman, Inc.: Bruce Coleman—88 (top), John S. Flannery—26 (top), K. Gunnar—108 (top), Norman Myers—73 (bottom), R. Vroom—70; Exxon—42-43; Nat Fain—119 (top), 123; Freelance Photographers Guild: Dennis L. Crow—130, Elisofon—72-73 (top), FPG—53 (bottom), Bob Gladden —139, Burton McNeely—97, Tom Myers—2-3, 37, 52, 84-85, Chuck Nicklin—124, J. Zimmerman—53 (top); Gary Haselau —28, 29; Bruce C. Heezen and Charles D. Hollister, *The Face of the Deep*, Oxford University Press, 1971—24 (bottom), 25, 32 (top); Huntington Beach News—50; C. P. Idyll—77 (top); *Los Angeles Times*—51; R. McAllister—110; James W. McBeth —98 (top); Jack McKenney—5; Richard C. Murphy—12, 71, 117 (bottom); Richard C. Murphy and Emmett Collins—140, 141; Musée Oceanographique de Monaco—112; F. G. Myers (courtesy of The World Life Research Institute)—126; Chuck Nicklin—107 (bottom); Photography Unlimited: Ron Church—107 (top); Carl Roessler—103; The Sea Library: California Fish and Game Department—88 (bottom right), B. Campoli—18, 32-33 (bottom), Jim Cooluris—92 (bottom), 118, Jack Drafahl—30-31 (top), 138 (top), B. Evans—92 (top left), Henry Genthe—138 (bottom), Global Marine Corporation—24 (top), George Green—95, William L. High—80-81, William L. High, National Marine Fisheries Service—78, 83, 90, 94, Bill MacDonald—75, Jack McKenney—64 (top) (middle), 65, Marine Photographic Association—38, Elliott Norse—91, Coles Phinizy—22, 23, Carl Roessler—7, 121, 125, James Scott—116 (top), Valerie Taylor—120, Paul Tzimoulis—64 (bottom), Steve Williams—21, Bill Yancey—122; Eugene A. Shinn—59, 67; Sodel Phototheque E.D.F.—46; Tom Stack & Associates: Ron Church—19 (bottom), 40 (top), E. R. Degginger—88 (bottom left), Al Giddings—89 (bottom), Keith Gillett—68, Bill Noel Kleeman—86-87 (bottom), Dave LaTouche—137 (bottom), Larry Moon—45, Orion Press—82, Kenneth R. H. Read— 117 (top), 119 (bottom), Tom Stack—142, Bob Wick—93, Eric Young—132-133; Surfer Publications, Inc.: Steve Wilkings —134-135; Taurus Photos: Don Dedera—36 (bottom), 39, C. P. Idyll—57, 76, 77 (bottom), 86 (top), 98-99 (bottom), C. B. Jones—36 (top), Robert Marx—15, Dave Woodward—106 (top), 137 (top); Herb Taylor—104, 105; Charles A. Turner, California Fish and Game Department—111; Myron Wang—115.